UNIVERSITY OF NOTRE DAME

Liturgical Studies

MADE, NOT BORN

NEW PERSPECTIVES ON
CHRISTIAN INITIATION AND THE CATECHUMENATE

Liturgical Studies

MADE, NOT BORN

New Perspectives on
Christian Initiation and the Catechumenate

F R O M
T H E M U R P H Y C E N T E R
F O R L I T U R G I C A L R E S E A R C H

UNIVERSITY OF NOTRE DAME PRESS

NOTRE DAME   LONDON

Aidan Kavanagh's "Christian Initiation of Adults: The Rites" originally appeared as an article in *Worship,* vol. 48 (1974), pages 318–335, and is reprinted here with permission.

Library of Congress Cataloging in Publication Data

Made, not born.

(Liturgical Studies)
Paper presented at a symposium sponsored by the
Murphy Center for Liturgical Research.
Bibliography: p.
Includes index.
1. Baptism—Addresses, essays, lectures.
2. Confirmation—Addresses, essays, lectures.
3. Lord's Supper—Addresses, essays, lectures.
4. Catechumens—Addresses, essays, lectures.
I. Murphy Center for Liturgical Research. II. Series:
Notre Dame, Ind. University. Liturgical
BV812.M27   265   75-19874
ISBN o-268-00708-X
ISBN 0-268-01337-3 pbk.

Manufactured in the United States of America

Contents

Acknowledgments

The Murphy Center wishes to acknowledge with gratitude the splendid leadership provided by its former director, the Reverend James D. Shaughnessy, which has brought this book to completion. We are likewise deeply indebted to the editorial expertise of Mr. Richard P. Humbrecht without whose care and industry this publication could never have been achieved. At the same time, the Center realizes with a similar sense of gratitude, that the labors of Mrs. Ann W. Lauer were altogether indispensable in this book's production.

September 25, 1975   John Gallen, S.J.
                                               Director
                                               Murphy Center for
                                                   Liturgical Research

Christian Initiation: Tactics and Strategy

Aidan Kavanagh, OSB

THE CLEAREST SYMPTOM OF THE PRESENT STATE OF THE CHURCH IS THE quality of recent discussion on the matter of Christian initiation. Questions are being asked, and answers given, about the right age for confirmation, about how best to catechize parents of infants brought for baptism, about whether infant baptism itself is a good thing,[1] about first confession for children baptized as infants, and so on. The discussion such questions and answers generate is for the most part a tactical one carried on by concerned pastors and a few others in face of declining church attendance, parochial schools going on the rocks, decreasing clerical and religious order labor pools, financial constriction all around, and a seeming disintegration in Church discipline and Christian witness.[2]

These concerned pastors and a few others are surely right in their reading of reports from the field. They are also right in sensing that Christian initiation has something to do with the reports coming in from the field. Yet I think they are only partially right—and being only partially right is a poignantly existential way of being wrong—in assuming that tactical responses to the perceived difficulties are adequate. The difficulties seem strategic, and only strategic responses will do.

One example may illustrate my point. The question "what age confirmation" is a tactical one; it is also perilously easy to answer tactically. Pick an age, any age: all can be defended, and any can be enforced if there is a will to do so and sufficient coercive power at hand. But it may be that while the question itself is tactical the reason for asking it is vastly strategic. Perhaps the reason for asking the question at all arises out of a generally sensed, if not yet

1

clearly defined, need for the Church to be more tough and candid about the Gospel of Jesus Christ with people at a time in people's lives when toughness and candor can do the most good for all concerned.

If this be the case, however, one may note that the issue raised concerns far more than the appropriate age at which a rite as intrinsically modest as confirmation is to be administered. The issue concerns *why* one should be confirmed at all, and *how* one gets to the point of even wanting confirmation. In other words, the issue embraces the whole of the Church's policy on who a Christian is and how he gets to be that way. Phrasing the question of confirmation tactically in terms of age, and responding to it tactically by giving one, not only turns over no rocks and flushes out none of the snakes that lurk there, but also confirms their territoriality and signals our own intent to avoid the area where solutions to our problems may lie hidden. For when we talk about confirmation our conversation is really about baptism; when we are dealing with baptism we are discoursing about Christian initiation; when we are into initiation we are face to face with conversion in Jesus Christ dead and rising; and when we are into conversion in Jesus Christ dead and rising we are at the storm center of the universe.

This is, I take it, something of what we mean by saying that sacraments cause in terms of what they signify: *sacramenta significando efficiunt gratiam*. This truism has two results which bear on the matters to be discussed in this volume. First, it underlines the fact that baptism, confirmation, and eucharist, neither in isolation from each other nor taken together as one complex whole, can go surrogate for the entire gamut of phenomena that make up Christian initiation. The new *Order of Christian Initiation of Adults,* published by the Holy See in January 1972 but not yet available for use in English, acknowledges as much by referring consistently to these three sacraments, not as "Christian initiation" as such, but as the *sacraments of initiation.*[3] Further it treats these as only one phase in the initiatory process, the other two being precatechumenal and catechumenal catechesis on one hand and postbaptismal catechesis on the other.

Second, the truism places squarely before us the fact that no sacrament can be adequately interpreted or celebrated without recourse to the whole, rich context of meaning out of which it arises. That whole, rich context of meaning is what constitutes the sacrament as sign, and it is only by *signifying* that a sacrament causes. *Sacramenta significando efficiunt gratiam,* said Trent, and Trent was right.[4] In the case of the sacraments of initiation their whole context of meaning is too rich and multiform to be reduced to a definition. I think, however, that its contours can be discerned in the biographical accounts of individual conversion in Jesus Christ dead and rising. One thinks of Paul's account of what happened on the road to Damascus, and of all that preceded and followed it. One also thinks of Augustine's *Confessions.*

In these and many other accounts one notices an imperceptibly growing realization that the normalcy of life lived within the conventions of one's own world is but the face of death itself. The realization finally reaches a focal point of intensity that will not be denied. Paul falls from his horse, Augustine hears a child singing. Time is suspended, things become still, there is a sense of fear and falling. Tears, desolation, and total disorientation of one's personal sense of goals and values follow, signalling perhaps the dissolution of one's former identity. Only then does one discover that in this whole process a new person has been coming to birth in one, that this new person, unrecognized, is now one's new self. At this point speech returns, sight returns; new things are said that were before unspeakable, new things are seen that were always there. Time expands with the speed of light, life begins for the first time, and there is something to sing about.

From precatechumenate and catechumenate through the sacraments of initiation and postbaptismal catechesis, Christian initiation as a whole ecclesial structure exists *to protect the Church* and *to protect the individual* undergoing such a trauma from the Church's insensitivity to the crisis. Further, it exists in order *to bring both the Church and the converting individual* into a mutually profitable relationship as a result of the trauma having occurred. This mutually profitable relationship is, on a sustained basis, what I conceive communion to be. Establishing such communion is the ultimate purpose of the whole initiatory process. Sustaining such communion beyond its initiatory phase is the ultimate purpose of the whole of Church order, the heart of which is the sacramental economy centering especially on the eucharist. One might say, in sacramental terms, that baptism and all it presupposes is the way the eucharist begins, and that the eucharist and all it causes is the way baptism is sustained. *Sacramenta significando efficiunt gratiam quam significant.* Sacraments by signifying cause the grace they signify.

This is, in brief, something of the strategic plateau from which I think we should view the tactical range of questions that confront us. Viewing the latter from the vantage point of the former opens up new possibilities for insight into problems that appear to have no solutions. For example, *catechesis* begins to appear more as a matter of conversion therapy than an exercise in "religious education."[5] *Baptism* begins to appear more as the communal watershed event that both signifies one's having come into communion with Jesus Christ dead and rising among his faithful people and causes that entrance to attain new levels of intensity. Baptism begins to appear less as a preliminary and rather "exorcistic" excision of infants from the power of evil and the jaws of hell. *Confirmation* begins to appear less as a brief ceremony of maturity in faith, or of puberty in early adolescence, and more as a solemn pneumatic conclusion to baptism that finally equips one for full sharing in the eucharistic celebration of a people filled with the Spirit of Jesus whom the Father sends as that people's living bond of unity. And finally, the Church itself begins to appear less as a static institution resistant to change, and more as an organic and power-laden mystery that is constantly coming into existence precisely through a change in people that is so radical it can only be described as a dying and a being born again. For this reason alone the Church cannot be regarded as merely something benign stuck onto the world from without. It is, instead, merely the world made new.

This is rich stuff, as bracing as it is ambiguous. In what follows in this volume it will no doubt be made much more concrete historically, theologically, and pastorally than I have time here. But I hazard that little of its richness, and even less of its ambiguity, will be dispelled. This should not frustrate us. Learning to live with rich ambiguity is not a fault but a virtue. It is the poverty of precision that is killing us.

I journeyed to London, to the timekept City,
Where the River flows, with foreign flotations.
There I was told: we have too many churches,
And too few chop-houses. There I was told:
Let the vicars retire. Men do not need the Church
In the place where they work, but where they spend their
*   Sundays.*
In the city we need no bells:
Let them waken the suburbs.
I journeyed to the suburbs, and there I was told:
We toil for six days, on the seventh we must motor
To Hindhead, or Maidenhead.
If the weather is foul we stay home and read the papers.
In industrial districts, there I was told
Of economic laws.
In the pleasant countryside, there it seemed
That the country now is only fit for picnics.
And the Church does not seem to be wanted
In country or in suburb; and in the town
Only for important weddings. [6]

Stop asking at what age confirmation should be administered; the question is when and under what conditions we should initiate a Christian. Stop asking at what age children should make their first confession; the question is what ecclesial effect sin has on communion in faith. Stop asking how much or how little doctrinal quantity the catechism ought to contain; the question is what is conversion and how does one survive it. Stop asking for federal funds to prop up educational programs; the question is what is catechumenate and how does it function. Stop asking what the sex of a minister ought to be; the question is what is Christian ministry, where has it gone, and why. Stop asking how the Church might better serve the world; the question is how the Church might better serve the imperative of the Gospel, and consequently aid this world in discovering itself made new in the Church itself.

The radical discovery of ourselves as Church is possible only in terms of Jesus dead and rising. Where this passage from death to life is continuously available to us is in the conversion of people actually passing from death to life in him, and by him, and through him among his faithful people. Christian initiation is this passage. It is we ourselves keeping faith, and we ourselves keeping faith is where this world is born anew in life everlasting.

Who does not know initiation does not know the Church. Who does not know the Church does not know the Lord. And who knows neither the Church nor the Lord does not know the world as God meant it to be from before always.

NOTES

1. See David Perrey, *Baptism at 21* (New York: Vantage Press, 1974).

2. See the United States Catholic Bishops' statement of concern on evangelism, *Origins* 4, no. 6 (July 4, 1974): 93–96. A recent poll of American leaders on the eighteen most powerful institutions rated "Organized Religion" last, after the Republican Party. Reported in *Commonweal* 100 (14 June 1974): 322.

3. Since this essay was written, the Provisional Text approved for interim use in the dioceses of the United States has been published. See *Rite of Christian Initiation of Adults, Provisional Text* (Washington, D.C.: United States Catholic Conference, 1974).

4. *Conc. Trid.*, session VII, canon 6 (*Enchiridion Symbol-orum*, ed. Denzinger-Rahner [1957]: para. 849). See also K. Rahner, *The Church and the Sacraments*, trans. W. J. O'Hara (New York: Herder and Herder, 1963): 34–40.

5. See my "Teaching Through the Liturgy," *Notre Dame Journal of Education* 5 (1974): 35–47.

6. T. S. Eliot, "Choruses from 'The Rock,'" *T. S. Eliot: Selected Poems*, (New York: Harbrace Paperbound Library 1936): 107–108.

CHAPTER I

Christian Initiation in the New Testament

Reginald H. Fuller

The origins of Christian baptism

MEMBERSHIP IN THE OLD ISRAEL WAS NEVER A MATTER OF NATURE OR OF birth per se. Israel was not the natural offspring of Yahweh but had been brought into being, adopted[1] by Yahweh to be his people. Israel was created by a particular *Heilsgeschichte* which entailed the inauguration of a covenant.[2] After the earliest generation each subsequent Israelite gained admission into this covenant and insertion into this *Heilsgeschichte* not by virtue of nature or birth, but by a special rite, the rite of circumcision.[3]

The growth of Israel's eschatological hope included the hope for a renewed people of God constituted by a new *Heilsgeschichte*, the messianic event. Although as early as Jeremiah the prophets had reinterpreted circumcision ethically, no indication appears that an eschatological circumcision was anticipated as the means of entry into the messianic salvation. It is only in the later stratum of the New Testament, in the deutero-Pauline Colossians, that baptism is described as a new eschatological or messianic circumcision, the *peritomē Christou*. The Paul of the homologoumena does not take this line.

If there is any theological preparation for Christian baptism in Jewish eschatology, it is to be sought rather in the concept that at the beginning of the messianic age Israel would recapitulate the experiences of the exodus period, and would therefore pass through the Red Sea again.[4] Paul seems to speak of such a tradition in I Corinthians where he draws a clear analogy between Israel passing under Moses through the Red Sea and the baptism of the Christian believers.[5] There is thus no direct line leading from Old Testament circumcision to Christian baptism, and the connection was drawn only in the subapostolic age. The most we can say is that circumcision provided the idea that membership of the people of God, whether under the old covenant or the new, is not by nature or birth but by insertion into a *Heilsgeschichte*.

The immediate external origin of Christian baptism is clearly the rite practiced by John the Baptist. It was from John that the movement launched by Jesus emerged. The source of Johannine baptism, however, is much controverted. A common view, still favored by English speaking scholars, is that John took over the Jewish practice of proselyte baptism and deliberately required it of Israelites.[6] Unfortunately, the first clear evidence for the practice of proselyte baptism is late, and like so much from the Mishnah it cannot be dated prior to 200 A.D. Of course, one can argue that by the time baptism had become the characteristic rite of Christian initiation, the Jewish community would not likely have adopted it. I must confess that I can find indications of proselyte initiation similar to its Christian counterpart only at the stage when the Hellenistic mission began, and here the influence is seen in the emergence of patterns of catechetical instruction[7] rather than in a sacramental rite.

An alternative suggestion is that John the Baptist created the batismal rite out of various prophetic utterances about a future eschatological cleansing.[8] But the evidence here is rather elusive.

During the period of Qumran fever it was thought that John the Baptist acquired his rite from Qumran.[9] The allusions to ritual ablutions in the texts,[10] the archeological evidence of the elaborate water supply at Qumran, and the geographical proximity of the Baptist to Qumran all seemed to point in this direction. The texts, however, do not speak of an initiatory baptism, but rather of daily ablutions. One might argue of course that there had to be a first moment when one started taking the daily bath in the community. But there is no indication that any particular significance was attached to this moment, still less is there any evidence that a theology of initiation gathered around such a rite.

It is for these reasons that German scholarship today favors the view that both Qumran and John the Baptist were manifestations of a widespread phenomenon in the Jordan area. Indeed, this view was propounded by L. Thomas nearly forty years ago.[11] But we must be clear about the difference between John the Baptist on the one hand and Qumran or the general baptist movement in Palestine and Syria on the other. John's baptism was riveted to his eschatology in a way that these other baptismal practices were not. John's baptism was a singular conversion event carrying with it the promise of eschatological salvation. Perhaps the best solution is to combine two of the theories already mentioned; John took over the baptism practice of Qumran or of the baptist sects in general and combined it with the prophetic idea of an eschatological cleansing before the End.

The synoptic gospels are silent as to whether Jesus practiced baptism. Morton Smith has recently propounded the thesis that Jesus was, among other things, the practitioner of secret initiatory rites involving water baptism.[12] If so, it is odd that the earliest traditions behind the synoptists (the preMarcan tradition, the Q material, the special Lucan and the special Matthean material) are completely silent on the subject. Although it contradicts itself on the subject, the Fourth Gospel seems to suggest that there was a period in Jesus' ministry when he did practice baptism,[13] but that this period was confined to the time when Jesus carried on a ministry parallel to that of the Baptist. Even the Fourth Gospel does not speak of Jesus' practice of baptism after he embarked on his own distinctive ministry—a period subsequent to John's imprisonment. If there was an interim period when Jesus baptized, it was one similar to Johannine baptism, not a distinctively Christian baptism. When Jesus began to assert that the reign of God was already breaking through, he apparently abandoned Johannine baptism, which merely pointed toward that coming reign and prepared men and women for it.

Nowhere do the gospels suggest that for Jesus, as for others whom John baptized, baptism signified repentence preparatory to the advent of the reign of God. On the other hand, the narratives of Jesus' baptism are clearly shaped by the Church's postPaschal Christology. The historical meaning of Jesus' baptism can be detected only from his attendant words and conduct. First, it was subsequent to his own baptism that Jesus embarked upon his eschatological mission, proclaiming the eruption of the eschatological reign of God.[14] As we have seen, there was probably a time lag between Jesus' baptism and the inauguration of his own independent mission. Yet Jesus regarded his own *exousia,* the authority by which he performed his own distinctive eschatological mission, as intimately bound up with that of John. Two synoptic sayings go so far as to suggest that Jesus spoke of his own death as a baptism.[15] Assuming the authenticity of these sayings,[16] Oscar Cullmann used them as the basis for the twin theses that Jesus understood his own baptism as the vocation to be the suffering servant, and interpreted his own death as a general baptism for all men. These synoptic sayings, however, would be viewed today by most critical scholars as creations of the post-Paschal community. Likewise, the theology of Jesus' death as a general baptism, if present in the texts at all, would be seen as a postPaschal creation. Since Jesus' baptism was his call to eschatological mission and since that mission included his death,[17] we can say in only the most general sense that Jesus' baptism implied his death. It would be unwise to erect as did Cullmann a whole theology of baptism upon this supposed interpretation by Jesus of his baptism.

Baptism in the Post-Paschal Community

The post-resurrection appearances established the eschatological community[18] consisting of Peter, the Twelve, and the five hundred. I have argued elsewhere[19] that these appearances involved also / an imparting of the Spirit—the hallmark of eschatological life—to all recipients.[20] But even if we follow the author of Acts in separating the gift of the Spirit from the appearances and reserve it exclusively for the foundation members of the community on Pentecost, it remains true that the foundation members did not receive baptism in the sense in which all others who entered the community did. Their baptism was, so to speak, their total immersion into the Christ event. It is noteworthy that Acts 1:5 characterizes the Pentecost event as a baptism with the Spirit, in accordance with a saying attributed to the risen Lord, but which evidently originated in a saying of the Baptist.[21] Like all the speeches of the risen One, this too will be later tradition rather than historical record, if not Lucan composition. Nevertheless, this may enshrine a primitive tradition that the early community interpreted the reception of the Spirit as the fulfillment of the Baptist's prophecy. Was this also what led that community to revive the Baptist's practice of baptism? Later tradition attributed this to an explicit command of the risen One.[22] Once again, the verbalizations of the post-resurrection encounters are comparatively late. But the widespread attestation of the baptismal theme in them, however, suggests that from quite early on the post-Paschal community understood its revival of the Johannine practice of water baptism with its new Christian meaning to be the result of the impact of the post-resurrection encounters, just like the kerygma itself. In this indirect sense we may ground the post-Paschal baptismal practice in the command of the risen One.

It is clear that for all who did not belong to the original nucleus which experienced the resurrection appearances, baptism was the universal means of entering the eschatological community. The thesis of the history-of-religions-school adopted by Kirsopp Lake,[23] —that baptism began first in the Hellenistic communities and that Acts 2:38 is an anachronism—is now generally abandoned, largely on the ground that Paul presupposes the universality of baptism.[24] Paul seems to include himself in this "we" and therefore the story of his own baptism would rest on historical fact.[25] I personally favor the opinion that Paul counted himself among the foundation members of the ecclesia[26] and that by seeing the risen One and receiving the gift of the Spirit in that appearance he was thus totally immersed directly in the Christ event and did not require water baptism. This would be consistent with his claims to be an apostle and to have received the gospel not through men but directly from Jesus Christ.[27] However that may be, it is clear that everyone who came after the original foundation event could establish contact with the eschatological reality brought in Christ only through hearing the kerygma, and could participate in that reality only through water baptism. Probably reflecting to some extent the ideas of his own local church, the author of Acts associates three meanings with baptism:

First, like Johannine baptism, it conveys ἀφεσις ἁμαρτιων, "forgiveness" (or better, "remission") of sins. According to Bultmann,[28] this was very likely true of Christian baptism from the very beginning.

Second, baptism was ἐπι το ὀνοματι Ἰησου χριστου. Since Paul presupposes this in his argument in I Corinthians 1:13, and 6:11 presupposes in the Hellenistic churches the custom of baptism "in the name of (the) Christ," this feature must be pre-Pauline. But was it only Hellenistic and not Palestinian? Bultmann[29] thought it could be traced back to the earliest community where, however, it was merely an exorcistic formula, and that only in the Hellenistic communities did this primitive exorcistic formula acquire a positive significance, setting up a "sacramental relation with the person of Jesus and putting him under the protection of his name."[30] It would surely be reasonable, however, to infer that baptism was understood from the earliest days as conveying all salvific consequences (so far as they were perceived at that date) which resulted from the saving event.

The third effect, somewhat loosely attached to baptism, is the gift of the Spirit. (Note how Peter's speech in Acts detaches the reception of the Spirit from baptism by the word και: Repent . . . be baptized . . . "and" (και) you shall receive the Holy Spirit. The Spirit is received temporally after baptism, but not necessarily instrumentally through baptism. This sequence of events seems to be reflected in the synoptic narratives of Jesus' baptism.) By detaching the reception of the Spirit from water baptism, the author of Acts to some extent prepares the way for those passages where the Spirit is detached completely from water baptism, either temporally preceding it or attached to a subsequent outward sign. How early was the reception of the Spirit associated with baptism? Bultmann thought it went back only to the Hellenistic communities.[31] This is unlikely. Käsemann's research[32] has established the earliest community as already characterized by pneumatic enthusiasm. I take it that the glossalalia at Pentecost belongs to the earliest tradition, and that therefore baptism was commonly followed by speaking in tongues. In the later Hellenistic church represented by Luke this has ceased to be the invariable norm.[33]

Another significant feature of baptism in the earliest community should be noted. Acts speaks of the baptized as being "added."[34] These references occur in summary passages, and in their present form they are the work of the author.[35] Moreover the verb προστίθημι is used in the Septuagint to signify admission into a community.[36] Since Septuagintalisms are a characteristic of Lucan style, we may accredit the phrase to Lucan composition. However I see no reason why he should not be reflecting much earlier ideas; baptism is an act whereby *God* adds believers to the eschatological community.[37] Baptism further brings one into an already existing community. One does not become a believer and then decide to form a society with other believers. Here, perhaps, we can see the importance of the resurrection appearances in relation to baptism. The resurrection appearances created the community. After hearing of the kerygma and faith, baptism is the means by which God inserts new members into the already existing community.

We have already mentioned the exceptional passages in Acts in which the reception of the Spirit is dissociated from water baptism. These are of two types. First, there is the case of Cornelius, where the illapse of the Spirit occurs between the acceptance of the kerygma and water baptism, the latter following as a consequence of the gift of the Spirit.[38] In the second reference, where Peter reports the episode to the Jerusalem church, no explicit reference to water baptism is made, but it is implied in the phase ἐγωητις μην δυνατος κωλυσαι νον θεον.[39] It is clear that Luke intends by this precedence of the Spirit's illapse before baptism to indicate that the mission to the gentiles was due to the divine initiative.[40] The episode has been aptly called the Pentecost of the Gentiles,[41] a point which Peter's speech at Jerusalem emphasizes.[42] It is generally agreed today that while the Cornelius story may rest upon an authentic episode in early Christian history, its significance has been blown out of all proportion by the author of Acts whose concern was to establish an apostolic imperative for the gentile mission. Since this prior illapse of the Spirit conforms with the Lucan theological concern, I am inclined to view that too as part of the Lucan composition. That he could do this indicates that by his own time the close attachment of the gift of the Spirit with baptism was beginning to be loosened.

The second type of exceptional passages in which the reception of the Spirit is dissociated from water-baptism raises additional problems, especially since it involves the separate sign of the laying on of hands following water baptism.[43] There is also this curious difference between the two passages: the first has the laying on of hands temporally detached from the water-baptism and administered by different persons (Peter and John instead of Philip, one of the seven), whereas in the second instance the laying on of hands follows immediately upon the water-baptism and is performed by the same minister (Paul). I take it that Luke is here presupposing the practice of his own church in which the laying on of hands had become an additional ceremony to baptism,[44] first clearly attested to outside the New Testament in Tertullian.[45] If this presupposition is in each case due to Lucan redaction, then these passages cannot be used as evidence for confirmation as an apostolic rite. These passages belong to the subapostolic phase of the initiation trajectory. The separation of the laying on of hands in Acts 8 has nothing to do with the western medieval separation of confirmation from baptism but is due rather to Luke's redactional interest in subordinating each successive new stage in the Christian mission to the Jerusalem church and its apostolate.

The Hellenistic Church Aside from Paul

We have hardly any literary remains of the Hellenistic Church prior to Paul. This is regrettable since this phase of early Christian history contributed notably to the development of early Christianity. Further it represents the milieu in which Paul was nurtured prior to his leaving the community at Antioch,[46] and an influence upon which he depended in part and against which he was in part reacting.

As in earliest Palestinian Christianity, the process of initiation began with the proclaiming of the kerygma and its reception in faith. But the kerygma had to begin with the Hellenistic Church, as it were, further back. No longer was it sufficient simply to proclaim the Christ event. Before that event could be announced it was necessary to establish faith in the one God.[47] Paul also hints at the beginnings of a catechumenate, reminding the Romans—a community which he had not founded—that they were given a pattern of teaching.[48] The parenetic sections of the Pauline epistles include sterotyped forms of teaching which may be precisely the kind of thing Paul is referring to here.[49] This teaching would include such items as the injunction to put off[50] the vices of pagan living (followed by a catalogue of vices) and to put on the Christian virtues (followed by a catalogue of these).[51] Perhaps this already attests to the attachment of a symbolic significance in the baptismal rite to the stripping off of one's garments and putting on a new baptismal robe—surely a necessity although the white robe is not mentioned until after the New Testament period.[52]

There are hymnic materials in the epistles which are widely ascribed to the baptismal liturgy of the Hellenistic missionary churches. Among these are the following:

In Christ Jesus (we) are all sons of God,
    through faith
For (we) who were baptised into Christ have
    put on Christ.
There is neither Jew nor Greek,
There is neither slave nor free,
There is neither male nor female,
For (we) are all one in Christ.[53]

(He) has qualified us to share in the inheritance
    of the saints in light.
He has delivered us from the dominion of darkness
    and transferred us to the kingdom of his
    beloved son,
In whom we have the redemption,
    the forgiveness of sins[54]

Awake, O sleeper, and arise from the dead,
And Christ shall give you light[55]

(We are) built into the spiritual house,
  to be a holy priesthood,
  to offer spiritual sacrifices
  acceptable to God through Jesus Christ.
(We) are a chosen race,
  a royal priesthood,
  a holy nation,
  God's own people,
that (we) may declare the wonderful deeds
  of him who called (us) out of darkness
  into his (own) marvelous light.

Once (we) were no people
  but now (we) are God's people;
once we had not received mercy
  but now we have received mercy.[56]

There is a whole wealth of imagery clustering round the baptismal rite as it was practiced in the Hellenistic missionary churches. Some of the imagery is rooted in the baptismal theology of the earliest Palestinian community.[57] Similarly, the early concept of baptism as establishing a special relation to Christ, enshrined in the formula of baptism into the name of Christ, is reflected in the expression of these special relationships: baptism is performed "in Christ";[58] we "put on" Christ; we become "one in Christ"; we are "translated into the kingdom of God's Son." In baptism it is Christ who gives us light.

But there are other notions which take us beyond the thinking of the earliest community so far as we can discern it. We have already noted the language of putting on (Christ), which was possibly derived from the actual baptismal ceremony in which a symbolic meaning was perhaps already given to the stripping and reclothing of the candidate. We also suggested that this language may have been derived from the language already current in Jewish proselyte baptism. Of a similar kind and perhaps of a similar origin is the language which speaks of the newly baptized as inheriting the prerogatives of the covenant people of God: adoption to sonship,[59] sharing the inheritance ($\kappa\lambda\eta\rho\omega\nu o\mu\iota a$, a word rooted in the notion of "the promised")[60] and transference from one sphere to another. This last is paschal language: the darkness/light contrast which appears in three of these hymns, the prerogatives of becoming the household, the holy or royal priesthood, the holy nation, the people of God's possession. It would be reasonable to suppose that this type of language was also derived from Jewish proselyte initiation as practiced in the diaspora.

There are also other ideas which seem to take us beyond either primitive Palestinian Christianity or Hellenistic Judaism. Such ideas are found in the hymns which speak of the transcendence of differences of race, class, and sex, or of baptism as involving (dying and) rising from the dead. Perhaps the notion of being in Christ may have a similar extraneous provenance. Those commentators who follow the history-of-religions-school ascribe these notions to the influence of gnosticism and the mystery religions.[61]

It is important to note that Paul indicates quite clearly[62] that he was not the first to give baptism the interpretation that it involved sharing the fate of the cult deity as in the mystery religions, for he is appealing to something which the Romans already knew ("do you not know?"). It is further suggested by these same scholars that the notion of baptism into the body of Christ[63] is of similar origin.[64] Note especially that in this latter passage the notion of the body is coupled with the transcendence of racial and class differences.[65] A mystery origin, finally, has been discerned in the notion entertained by some at Corinth that vicarious baptism for the dead could enable them to participate in resurrection, that is, in the fate of the cult deity.[66] Conservative scholars have of course been at pains to deny the influence of the mystery religions or of gnosis at these points.[67] But the following qualifications should be noted. First, the apostle Paul is concerned to correct certain aspects of these mystery notions, a correction which is also shared, although to a lesser degree, by the deutero-Pauline writings. Second, the earlier view of the history-of-religions-school that baptism as such originated from the mystery religions is definitely untenable; it was universal in Palestinian Christianity from the beginning. It is simply a matter of extraneous influences enriching the baptismal theology of the earliest communities. Yet this enrichment does no more than to draw out the implication of the earliest baptismal theology that it was performed for the remission of sins and the imparting of the spirit.

Where these new interpretations went beyond the drawing out of implications and assimilated questionable elements of substance, they were subject to Pauline correction.

The Pauline Homologoumena

Paul inherited the baptismal theology of the Hellenistic missionary communities, but corrected it at decisive points to coincide with his cross-centered christology and his eschatological reservation (the "not yet"). In the Galatians hymn, he probably added the name "Jesus" to "Christ" in the phrase, "in Christ *Jesus* you are all the sons of God." For Paul, "Jesus" is the incarnate, crucified one whose fleshly life and crucifixion is not done away with by the resurrection, but rendered ever present.[68] Baptism does not take us beyond the cross to the resurrection but rather plunges us into a life constantly marked by the cross, by suffering, and by the eschatological reservation. Paul also probably added to the same hymn the phrase, "through faith," thus guarding against the magical notions of the mysteries.

When the Corinthians were saying "I belong to Paul, to Apollos or to Cephas or to Christ," the Apostle retorted, "Were you baptized into the name of Paul?" This suggests that Corinthians were indulging in mystery thinking, for in the mysteries the initiate was brought into a special personal relationship with the mystagogue. Paul countered this by saying that he did not appear among them primarily as a minister of baptism, but as a herald of the gospel:

> Were you baptized in the name of Paul? I am thankful that I baptized none of you except Crispus and Gaius; lest any one should say that you were baptized in my name. (I did baptize also the household of Stephanas. Beyond that I do not know whether I baptized any one else.) For Christ did not send me to baptize but to preach the gospel.[69]

This passage appears to be a Pauline depreciation of the significance of baptism. But elsewhere he took it with utmost seriousness. Probably his normal practice was to leave the administration of baptism to his subordinates, as a later bishop might delegate the actual baptism to his presbyters or deacons. Paul's purpose at

Corinth was, perhaps, precisely to avoid suggesting that a special relationship was being set up between the initiate and the mystagogue as in the mystery rites. Baptism was not for Paul a thing in itself; it derived its whole meaning from the gospel of which it was the enactment and effective representation. Here Paul reasserts the teaching of the earliest community, for which baptism was an effective representation of the kerygma, against Hellenistic corruptions.

In I Corinthians 10, Paul was arguing against the libertinist inferences which some of the Corinthians had drawn from baptism as a result of their mystery thinking. They thought that through baptism they had already been made partakers in the resurrection life and that therefore they were free from moral obligations. But for Paul baptism meant obedient commitment to the Lordship of Christ. He therefore offered a typological analogy:

> I want you to know, brethren, that our fathers were all under the cloud, and all passed through the sea, and all were baptized into Moses in the cloud and in the sea.[70]

In the first instance, it seems probable that Paul was drawing upon a typology already current in Hellenistic Christianity. There are two reasons for this. First, the idea of the Israelites' crossing of the Red Sea as a baptism may have its roots in Jewish eschatological expectations,[71] and it may have passed from there into both the theology of Jewish proselyte baptism and into the baptismal theology of the pre-Pauline Hellenistic mission. Second, the other part of the analogy, the manna/eucharistic typology, is not peculiar to Paul but reappears in Johannine thought[72] and may even be present in the synoptic feeding narratives. Both ideas would seem to be rooted in the liturgies of the Hellenistic Churches. But once again Paul makes his own distinctive use of the analogies in criticism of the Corinthian theology. The analogy contains a warning: "These things were written down for our instruction, upon whom the end of the ages has come." The 'sacraments' of the wilderness committed Israel to obedience to its Lord, and those who disobeyed through idolatry, sexual license, putting God to the test, and grumbling, were destroyed. Baptism commits us to obedience; it does not guarantee salvation.

In I Corinthians 12, Paul is ready to accept the Hellenistic theology of baptism as an incorporation into the body of Christ, a notion which probably had a gnostic origin. One was incorporated into the body of the gnostic redeemer: "We were all baptized into one body." Baptism thus sets up an ontological reality: "You *are* the body of Christ." Paul accepts this theology. But the Corinthians, once more, were drawing gnostic consequences from this ontological fact. They thought they were immune from the demands of agape, especially to the weaker brethren who lacked the spectacular charisms. So Paul qualifies this gnostic-derived ontological ecclesiology by introducing the Stoic analogy of the relationship between the community and the human body[73] in order to drive home the mutual responsibility which all in the community have for one another. Thus once again he stresses the obligation which baptism entails.

We have already noted the passage[74] in which Paul refers to vicarious baptism, suggesting that it, too, has its origins in the mystery religions. We may regret that Paul did not stop to correct this notion. The fact is that he was preoccupied with another question—the future expectation of a resurrection from the dead— and simply referred to the practice in an *argumentum ad hominem*. But the whole argument of I Corinthians 15 does have a relation to the doctrine of baptism, as is apparent in Romans 6. The resurrection life to which baptism purportedly admits the believers is consummated only at the parousia. The Corinthians thought that they were resurrected in baptism and that there was, therefore, no need for a resurrection from the dead.

In Romans 6 Paul makes this point explicit. It has been frequently pointed out by some commentators,[75] though the point is overlooked by others,[76] that all the verbs which speak of the believers' dying with Christ are in the aorist or perfect, whereas the verbs which speak of their rising again with him are imperatives, subjunctives, or futures:

> Do you not know that all of us who have been baptized into Christ Jesus were baptized ($\dot{\epsilon}\beta\alpha\pi\tau\iota\sigma\theta\eta\mu\epsilon\nu$, aorist) into his death? We were buried ($\sigma\upsilon\nu\epsilon\tau\alpha\phi\eta\mu\epsilon\nu$, aorist) therefore with him by baptism into death, so that as Christ was raised from the dead by the glory of the Father (not: "we have been raised," but:), we too might walk ($\pi\epsilon\rho\iota\pi\alpha\tau\eta\sigma\omega\mu\epsilon\nu$, aorist subjunctive) in newness of life.
> For if we have been united with him ($\gamma\epsilon\gamma o\nu\alpha\mu\epsilon\nu$, perfect) in a death like his, we shall ($\dot{\epsilon}\sigma o\mu\epsilon\theta\alpha$, future) certainly be united

with him in a resurrection like his. We know that our old self was crucified (συνεσταυρωθη aorist) with him so that the sinful body might be destroyed, and we might no longer be enslaved to sin. . . . But if we have died with Christ, we believe that we shall also live (ζησωμεν, future) with him. . . . So you also must consider yourselves (λογιζεσθε, imperative) dead to sin and alive to God in Christ Jesus.

In addition to the tenses of the verbs, two other features of Paul's language should be noted. First, the introduction of the element of faith in connection with the resurrection of the believers: they must *believe* that they might also live with him, and they must *consider* themselves alive to God in Jesus Christ. Second, there is the moral element: to die with Christ means not simply to share the fate of the cult deity, it means the initiation of a process of dying to sin (note that Paul did not say that we have already died to sin) and of walking in the newness of life. Resurrection of the believers takes place first at the parousia.

The Deutero-Pauline and Early Catholic Literature

The Pauline antilegomena tend to relax somewhat the severity of Paul's anti-gnostic and anti-mystery position, and to fall back upon the commonly accepted position of the Hellenistic missionary communities as expressed especially in baptismal hymns. In fairness, however,[77] they do retain something of the Pauline reservations.

Colossians cites what Dibelius[78] takes to be another baptismal hymn:

> In him also you were circumcised
>   with a circumcision made without hands,
> by putting off the body of flesh
>   in the circumcision of Christ;
> and you were buried with him in baptism,
> in which you were also raised with him
>   . . . from the dead.[79]

This passage reflects several differences from the Pauline homologoumena. First, baptism is regarded as a new circumcision. In Romans and Galatians circumcision was treated as the antithesis of the gospel, done away with in Christ. Here circumcision provides a suitable analogy to baptism: the fulfillment of the prophetic vision of a spiritual circumcision. Baptism is the circumcision of Christ—a Christian circumcision. The symbolism of stripping off, applied earlier to the idea of laying aside the vices of paganism, is now extended by means of the circumcision analogy to the putting off of the body of the flesh. Second, in baptism the believers are not only buried with Christ, they are actually raised with him—the very point which Romans refused to make. It is quite likely that Romans 6 presupposed just such a hymn. But whereas in Romans the resurrection side of the baptismal theology was corrected by the imperatives, subjunctives, and futures, here in Colossians the aorist is allowed to stand: συνεγερθητε, "you were raised." It looks as if Colossians has completely abandoned the reservations of Romans 6. But it must be noted that the deutero-Pauline author later modifies this outright mystery interpretation by means of a condition and an imperative: "If you then have been raised with Christ[80] seek[81] those things which are above."[82] If resurrection is now something already attained in baptism, it still obligates us to obey an imperative. A similar perspective is maintained with regard to the baptismal death: "If with Christ you died to the elemental spirits of the universe, why do you live as if you still belonged to the world?"[83]

Although Ephesians 2:1–6 does not explicitly mention baptism, it does appear to have baptismal overtones and may in fact draw upon further hymnic material from a baptismal liturgy:

> And you he made alive
> When you were dead through the trespasses and sins in which
>   you once walked . . .
> Among these we all once lived . . .
> and so we were by nature children of wrath . . .
> But God, who is rich in mercy,
> out of the great love with which he loved us,
> even when we were dead through our trespasses,
> made us alive together with Christ . . .
> and raised us up with him,
> and made us sit with him in the heavenly places.[84]

We see here the typical baptismal contrast between the old life and the new. It is once more the theme of dying and rising again with Christ. As in Colossians, the verbs of resurrection are in the aorist (συνεξωοποιησεν, συνηγειρεν, συνεκαθισεν). These aorists are left uncorrected. In fact, Ephesians seems to go further in a mystery-religion direction by asserting that through baptism the believers not only share Christ's resurrection but also his ascension: they are made to sit with him in the heavens. There could hardly be a more unqualified statement of the mystery-religion notion of sharing the fate of the cult deity. And yet the imperative and the eschatological reservation are not completely overlooked. Ephesians strongly affirms the notion of the believers' growing into what they already are through baptism. The believers are created in Christ Jesus for good works, in which God has prepared that they should walk. [85] They still have to continue to grow into a holy temple.[86] Their growth is still a matter for prayer.[87] There is a "not yet," an "until": "*until* we all attain to the unity of the faith and of the knowledge of the Son of God (the Corinthians too believed they already had gnosis), to mature manhood, to the measure of the stature of the fullness of Christ."[88] Above all, chapters four to six reaffirm the baptismal parenesis.

Finally, we have what looks like a fragment of baptismal hymn in II Timothy 2:11.[89] But if this is a baptismal hymn, then it has been corrected in accordance with the stricter Pauline notion of the futurity of the resurrection:

(For) if we have died with him
　　we shall also live ($συζησομεν$, future) with him
If we endure,
　　we shall also reign ($συμβασιλευσομεν$, future) with him.

It is surprising to find here that the hymn itself, which probably had mystery origins, has been corrected in accordance with strict Pauline notion. In this point the author of the Pastorals is a loyal Paulinist.

Perhaps the earliest use of the language of rebirth in connection with baptism is also found in the Pastorals, for in Titus 3:5 baptism is described as the "washing of regeneration." This language, like that of sharing the fate of the cult deity, was almost certainly derived from the mysteries.[90] Of course, it is also a natural development of the eschatological language of the earlier New Testament as when Paul speaks of the Christians as a new creation,[91] an idea seemingly based on the Jewish eschatological principle of *Urzeit gleich Endzeit*. But the language of rebirth goes beyond the Pauline language and is paralleled in the mystery texts, and so these latter must be the source of the development. However, the mystery parallels do not disclose the theological meaning of the Christian use. That lies in primitive Christian eschatology. Dibelius[92] specifies two major differences between the mystery and Christian concepts of παλιγγενεσια: absence of ecstasy in the Christian usage, and the corporate nature of the experience.[93]

That this rebirth language is not a peculiarity of the Pauline school is indicated by its fairly widespread occurrence. It is found in I Peter, a document which is thought to have baptismal associations:[94]

> By his great mercy we have been *born anew* to a living hope through the resurrection of Jesus Christ from the dead (1:3)
> Like *newborn babes,* long for the pure spiritual milk (2:2)

Finally there is John 3:3 and 5:

> Unless one is born anew (or: from above),
> he cannot see the kingdom of God (v. 3)
> Unless one is born of water and the Spirit,
> he cannot enter the kingdom of God (v. 5).

The most probable solution to the problem of the history of the tradition is that we have here an original eschatological saying of Jesus[95] reinterpreted by the Johannine school in terms of the developing concept of sacramental mystery.

In summary, there can be no doubt that Hellenistic Christianity developed its theology of baptism beyond the stage it had reached in earliest Palestinian Christianity. There was an eschatological sacrament conveying the eschatological blessings inaugurated by the Christ event (baptism in the name of Jesus, remission of sins, and reception of the Spirit). In Hellenistic Christianity it had become the sacrament of dying and rising again (sharing the fate of the cult deity) and later of rebirth. In addition there was the idea of admission to all the prerogatives of the covenant people of God, an idea which possibly was taken over from the similar theology of Jewish proselyte baptism.

The Holy Spirit and Baptism

Apparently Paul still knew nothing of a separate rite or sacramental action conveying the Spirit. The first text to note is I Corinthians 6:11:

You were washed, you were sanctified, you were justified in the name of the Lord Jesus Christ and in the Spirit of our God.

The verb ἀπολουσασθε and the phrase "in the name of the Lord Jesus Christ" show quite clearly that the apostle is speaking of baptism.[96] The word "sanctified" and the phrase "in the Spirit of our God" indicate that in baptism the believers were consecrated by the Spirit and so became ἅγιοι.

The second passage is II Corinthians 1:21–22:

It is God who establishes us (NEB, Gr· χρισας) . . . He has put his seal (σφραγισαμενος) upon us and given us his Spirit in our hearts as a guarantee.

Although baptism and water are not mentioned, the verbs χριω and σφραγιζω show that the passage refers to baptism. The verb χριω is used of the messianic anointing of Jesus at his baptism. [97] The noun χρισμα is used of the Christians, probably in reference to baptism,[98] and its origin seems to be the christological development of the narrative of the Lord's baptism. Originally dated at the exaltation,[99] the messianic anointing has been pushed back to the baptism, and as a result the baptismal narrative became a model for what happened to the Christians in their baptism. Similarly, the verb σφραγιζω is used in connection with Jesus' appointment to his messianic office,[100] probably at his baptism, and was then extended to the experience of Christians. [101] The connection of the sealing with baptism is therefore unmistakable. [102] In baptism, as by an instrument, the faithful receive the mark of God, the stamp of his eschatological ownership.

Thus there is no clear evidence that Paul knew a separate rite or part of a rite, such as anointing or laying on of hands, to mark this sealing with the Spirit. [103] But the two passages in Acts [104] and the one in Hebrews [105] seem to suggest that the laying on of hands was being introduced in the sub-apostolic age as an accompanying rite to water baptism.

The two chrism passages in John [106] do not refer explicitly to the Spirit, but many commentators suppose that this is what the writer had in mind. [107] Was he thinking of an actual anointing, or was he using the metaphorical language of water baptism? It is impossible to say, but it is easy to see how the metaphor would later develop into an accompanying rite, perhaps first among the gnostics. [108] Laying on of hands and/or anointing would not, of course, be a separate "sacrament," nor in the light of the New Testament evidence can they be said to be necessary over and above water-baptism. They can be a desirable underlining and expression of the total, rich meaning of water-baptism, but no more. As in so much of the history of early Christian thought and practice, the latest stratum of the New Testament stops somewhere along the line of an ongoing trajectory. The New Testament is an incomplete book which points beyond itself to further development.

NOTES

1. Cf. R. Fuller, "Adopt, Adoption," *A Theological Wordbook of the Bible*, ed. by A. Richardson (London: SCM Press, 1950).

2. There are in the Pentateuch two basic covenants in Israel's salvation history: that with Abraham, of which there are two versions in Gen. 15 (J) and Gen. 17:1–14 (P), and that with Moses in Exod. 21 ff.

3. The origins of circumcision are shrouded in antiquity. Theologically it was first associated with Moses (Exod. 4: 24–26 J). In P it was associated with Abraham (Gen. 17:9–27). After the exile it became the indispensable rite of initiation into the covenants of Israel.

4. J. Jeremias, *Infant Baptism in the First Four Centuries*, tr. D. Cairns (London: SCM Press, 1960): 31–32.

5. 1 Cor. 10:2.

6. See W. F. Flemington, *The New Testament Doctrine of Baptism* (London: S.P.C.K., 1957): 3–11. H. Strack and P. Billerbeck collected the relevant rabbinic references to proselyte baptism in their *Kommentar zum Neuen Testament*, (Munich: Beck, 1922): 102–106. Those like Flemington and Jeremias who support the view that Johannine and/or Christian baptism are derived from Jewish proselyte baptism rely on the materials collected by Billerbeck. The earliest references to the practice date back to the age of Hillel and Shammai, i.e., to the early first century. In *Holy Baptism: Supplement to Prayer Book Studies* 26, (New York: Church Hymnal Corporation, 1973): 16, D. B. Stevick cautiously stated that "Christian Baptism *probably, but not quite certainly*, found a model in Jewish proselyte baptism" (italics mine).

7. See P. Carrington, *The Primitive Christian Catechism* (Cambridge: University Press, 1940). This valuable work overemphasized the Palestinian Jewish origins of the catechetical pattern, much of which seems rather to have entered Hellenistic Judaism via the LXX and Stoicism. An earlier study of this subject was A. Seeberg, *Der Katechismus der Urchristenheit*, (Leipzig: Deichert, 1903).

8. G. W. H. Lampe, *The Seal of the Spirit* (London: Longmans, 1951): 25–27.

9. F. M. Cross, *The Ancient Library at Qumran* (New York: Doubleday, 1958): 70 and fn. 96a, 77, thought that the Qumran community practiced an

initiatory baptism. With slightly more caution, J. A. T. Robinson, "John the Baptist and the Qumran Community," *Twelve New Testament Studies,* Studies in Biblical Theology 34 (London: SCM Press, 1962): 11–17, proposed this derivation of Johannine baptism from the Qumran lustrations.

10. The crucial passage which speaks of entry into the covenant at Qumran is IQS 5:8–33. The reference to a water rite is ambiguous: "Let not the wicked enter the water to touch the Purification of the Holy." Is this entry a reference to an ongoing lustration or to a single initiatory rite?

11. L. Thomas, *Le mouvement baptiste en Palestine et Syrie* was published in 1935. It has not been accessible to me and I do not know what contemporary evidence (as opposed to later Mandaean etc.) he offered. Thomas' view was cited favorably by R. Bultmann, *Theology of the New Testament* I (London: SCM Press, 1951): 40 and by G. Bornkamm, *Jesus of Nazareth* (New York: Harper, 1960): 47 and fn. 31.

12. M. Smith, *A Secret Gospel* (New York: Harper, 1973): 97–101.

13. John 3:22; 4:1–2.

14. Cf. Mark 1:15. The language is that of the Hellenistic mission and the summary Marcan redaction, but the essential core, ἐγγικεν 'η βασιλεια certainly goes back to Jesus; it and similar formulations appear in Q, and it encapsulates the message of Jesus' parables.

15. Mark 10:39; Luke 12:50. Although Bultmann denied that the death of Jesus was integral to his mission, his pupils and others who launched and pursued the so-called New Quest have for various reasons asserted the integral place of Jesus' death in both his self-understanding and understanding of his mission. See J. M. Robinson, *A New Quest of the Historical Jesus,* Studies in Biblical Theology 25 (London: SCM Press, 1959): 121–125; E. Fuchs, *Studies of the Historical Jesus,* Studies in Biblical Theology 42 (London: SCM Press, 1964): 25–26; L. E. Keck, *A Future for the Historical Jesus* (Nashville: Abingdon, 1971): 228–231; P. E. Hodgson, *Jesus, Word and Presence* (Philadelphia: Fortress Press, 1971): 202–214.

16. O. Cullmann, *Baptism in the New Testament,* tr. J.K.S. Reid, Studies in Biblical Theology 1 (London: SCM Press, 1950): 19–20.

17. Mark 11:27–33. N. Perrin, *A Modern Pilgrimage in Christology* (Philadelphia: Fortress Press, 1974): argues that the theme of Jesus' ἐξουσια first entered the synoptic tradition via the Marcan redaction. Perrin, however, rested his case mainly on the Son of man saying in Mark 2:10 and did not mention Mark 11:27–33, where the theme of ἐξουσια belongs to the body of the pericope and is integral to it. Moreover, the theme, if not the actual word ἐξουσια, occurs in the independent Johannine version of the same pericope at John 2:18.

18. For the church-founding significance of the first three resurrection appearances see R. H. Fuller, *The Formation of the Resurrection Narratives* (New York: Macmillan, 1971).

19. R. H. Fuller, "The Resurrection of Jesus Christ," *Biblical Research* 4 (1960): 8–24, esp. 21.

20. Cf. John 20:19–23.

21. E. Haenchen, *The Acts of the Apostles* (Philadelphia: Westminster Press, 1971): 142.

22. Matt. 28:19 and Mark 16:16, but also the baptismal language of Luke 24:47 and John 21:23.

23. F. M. Foakes-Jackson and K. Lake (eds.), *The Beginnings of Christianity* I (London: Macmillan, 1920): 332–344, esp. 340.

24. Cf. Rom. 6:3–7.

25. It is indicative of the shift of opinion in this matter that Rudolf Bultmann, himself a product of the History of Religions school, took this position in *Theology* I, p. 39.

26. Cf. 1 Cor. 15:8.

27. Cf. Gal. 1:11–12.

28. Rudolf Bultmann, *Theology* I, p. 39.

29. *Ibid.*, p. 40.

30. *Ibid.*

31. *Ibid.*, pp. 137–138. In the discussion of baptism in the earliest church nothing was said of the Spirit (pp. 39–40).

32. E. Käsemann, "The Beginnings of Christian Theology," *New Testament Questions of Today* (Philadelphia: Fortress Press, 1969): 82–107.

33. Haenchen, *Acts*, pp. 172–174.

34. Cf. Acts 2:41, 47; 5:14. See also 11:24 at Antioch under Barnabas.

35. Haenchen, *Acts*, p. 195.

36. C. Maurer, *Theological Dictionary of the New Testament* VIII, ed. Gerhard Friedrich, tr. and ed. Geoffrey W. Bromiley (Grand Rapids: Wm. B. Eerdmans, 1972): 168.

37. *Ibid.*, fn. 28, compare the reverential passive in 2:41 with κυριος as subject of the active verb in 2:47.

38. Cf. Acts 10:44–48; 11:14–18.

39. Cullmann, *Baptism*, pp. 72–74.

40. Haenchen, *Acts*, p. 362.

41. Lampe, *Seal*, p. 66, "a second, purely Gentile Pentecost."

42. Cf. Acts 11:17

43. Cf. Acts 8:14–17; 19:5–6.

44. Cf. Hebrews 6:2.

45. Tertullian, *De Baptismo* 8. *Tertullian's Homily on Baptism*, ed. and tr. Ernest Evans (London: S.P.C.K., 1964).

46. British scholarship especially has tended to exaggerate the influence of Rabbinic Judaism on Pauline thought. It is often forgotten that Paul's formative years as a Christian were spent in communities of the Hellenistic Jewish Christian mission. See Bultmann, *Theology* I, pp. 187–189.

47. Cf. 1 Thess. 1:9.

48. Cf. Rom. 6:17.

49. For the patterns of teaching see Carrington, *Catechism*, pp. 61–65; M. Dibelius, "An die Kolosser Epheser An Philemon," Rev. H. Greeven, *Handbuch zum Neuen Testament* 12 (Tübingen: Mohr, 1953): 48–50.

50. ἀποτιθημι: see Carrington, *Catechism*, p. 61.

51. ἐνδυειν: see *Ibid.*, and fnn. 4 and 5.

52. Cf., however, Rev. 19:8.

53. Gal. 3:28. For the hymnic character of this fragment see R. Scroggs, "Paul and the Eschatological Woman," *Journal of the American Academy of Religion* 40 (1972): 283–303, esp. 328, following H. Schlier, *Der Brief an die Galater*, Meyer's Commentary 7 (Göttingen: Vandenhoeck & Ruprecht, 1962): 174–175.

54. Cf. Col. 1:12–14. For the hymnic character see J. M. Robinson, "Die

Hodayot-Formel in Gebet und Hymnus des Frühchristentumns," W. Eltester and F. Ketteler (eds.), *Apophoreta, Festschrift für Ernest Haenchen*, Beihefte zur Zeitschrift für die neutestamentliche Wissenschaft und die Kunde der älteren Kirche 30 (Berlin: Töpelmann; 1964): 231–232.

55. Cf. Eph. 5:14. The Greek editions of the New Testament (Nestle: Bible Societies') print this passage in verse form. The introductory λεγει shows clearly that it is a quotation. H. Schlier, *Der Brief an die Epheser* (Düsseldorf: Patmos, 1967): 240 followed E. Peterson in designating it as "lieber ein Kultspruch als ein Hymnus," but both agreed on its mystery origin.

56. Cf. 1 Peter 2:10. A hymnic origin for 1 Peter 2:4–10 was argued by G. S. Selwyn, *The First Epistle of St. Peter* (London: Macmillan, 1946): 277–281. Selwyn was clearly mistaken, however, in including the stone testimonies within the hymn as is clear from their very prosaic form and christological content.

57. As for instance when the Colossian hymn uses the quite un-Pauline language of the forgiveness of sins (άφεσις 'αμαρτιων) or the I Peter hymn the language of mercy; or the eschatological language of the kingdom, again in Colossians.

58. I have discussed the significance of the formula "In Christ" elsewhere. See R. H. Fuller, "Aspects of Pauline Christology," *Review and Expositor* 71, no. 1 (1974):5–17, esp. 10–11.

59. Cf. Gal. 3:28.

60. Cf. Col. 1:12.

61. E.g., Bultmann, *Theology* I, pp. 140–144.

62. Rom. 6:3.

63. 1 Cor. 12:13.

64. See E. Käsemann, *Leib und Leib Christi* (Tübingen: Mohr, 1933).

65. Cf. Gal. 3:28.

66. H. Lietzmann, *An die Korinther I, II*, Handbuch zum Neuen Testament 9 (Tübingen: Mohr, 1923): 83.

67. See esp. G. Wagner, *Pauline Baptism and the Pagan Mysteries*, trans. J. B. Smith (Edinburgh: Oliver & Boyd, 1967), *passim*.

68. See R. H. Fuller, "Aspects of Pauline Christology," pp. 6–8.

69. 1 Cor. 1:13–16.

70. 1 Cor. 10:1–2.

71. See Jeremias, *Infant Baptism*, p. 32.

72. Cf. John 6.

73. 1 Cor. 12:14–26.

74. 1 Cor. 15:29.

75. The following commentators call attention to the futures and subjunctives in Rom. 6:3–11; C. K. Barrett, *The Epistle to the Romans* (London: Black, 1959); K. Barth, *The Epistle to the Romans* (London: Oxford University Press, 1933).

76. R. Schnackenburg, *Baptism in the Thought of St. Paul* (Oxford: Blackwell, 1964): 32–45.

77. Bultmann and his school have not always been fair to the antilogoumena. See W. Marxsen, *Introduction to the New Testament*, trans. A. W. Buswell (Philadelphia: Fortress Press, 1968): 183, 196–198.

78. Dibelius, *Kolosser*, p. 31, who speaks of the "hymnartige Monotonie" of Col. 2:9—12.

79. Col. 2:11—12.

80. Conditional aorist, συνηγερθητε·.

81. Imperative, ζητειτε.

82. Col. 3:1.

83. Col. 2:20.

84. For the liturgical-hymnic character of this material see Dibelius, *Epheser*, p. 67.

85. Eph. 2:10.

86. Eph. 2:22.

87. Eph. 3:14—19.

88. Eph. 4:13.

89. M. Dibelius, *Die Pastoralbriefe* Handbuch zum Neuen Testament 13 (Tübingen: Mohr, 1955): 81 refers to this passage as "ein in hymnischem Stil gehaltenes Zitat unbekannter Herkunft."

90. Dibelius, *Pastoralbriefe*, pp. 111—113.

91. 2 Cor. 5:17.

92. Dibelius, *Pastoralbriefe*, p. 113.

93. "Die Wiedergeburt ist nicht nur dem einzelnen Mysten möglich; sie ist vielmehr das grundlegende Ereignis für alle Christen." See above, fn. 92.

94. F. L. Cross, *I Peter, a Paschal Liturgy* (London: Mowbray, 1954), and others (H. Preisker, M. E. Boismard) thought in terms of a baptismal liturgy. For a critique of this theory see T. C. G. Thornton, "I Peter, a Paschal Liturgy?" *Journal of Theological Studies*, New Series 12 (1961): 14—26. Others have suggested a baptismal homily, e.g., W. Bornemann, "Der erste Petrusbrief - eine Taufrede des Sylvanus?" *Zeitschrift für die neutestamentliche Wissenschaft* 19 (1919—1920): 143—165. A more cautious and acceptable view was expressed by Jeremias, *Infant Baptism*, p. 30: "we do not see in this letter a working over of a baptismal homily or even of a baptismal liturgy. We prefer to explain the numerous instances of baptismal terminology by the theory that the letter was addressed to the new converts of a recently completed missionary drive" (translation altered by me).

95. C. H. Dodd, *Historical Tradition in the Fourth Gospel* (Cambridge: University Press, 1963): 358—359.

96. H. Lietzmann, *Korinther*, p. 27.

97. Acts 4:27; 10:28. Luke 4:18. Heb. 1:9.

98. Cf. I John 2:10, 27.

99. Acts 2:36.

100. John 6:27.

101. Cf. Eph. 3:14; 4:30. Rev. 7:3—8.

102. *Contra* L. S. Thornton, *Confirmation; its Place in the Baptismal Mystery* (Westminster: Dacre Press, 1954), who erected upon a precariously speculative typology the thesis that in the New Testament sealing always refers to an additional rite. Like other writers of the same school he is never clear whether this other rite is the laying on of hands or anointing. See esp. pp. 33—38, 65—72, 88—197.

103. Nor despite Schlier is this clear in Eph. 1:13. H. Schlier, *Epheser*, p. 70.

104. Acts 8, and 19.

105. Heb. 6:2.

106. John 2:20, 27.

107. See the discussion in C. H. Dodd, *The Johannine Epistles*, The Moffatt New Testament Commentary (London: Hodder and Stoughton, 1946): 58–64.

108. Lampe, *Seal*, pp. 120–130.

CHAPTER II

Development of
the Christian Catechumenate

Robert M. Grant

ALTHOUGH SOME OF THE HISTORICAL DETAILS ARE COMPLICATED, THE thesis of this paper is quite simple. It involves some measure of assent to the presupposition that a doctrine of theological or liturgical evolution which produces a picture of straight-line development in the past does not do justice to the complexity of historical evidence and simply consecrates the present situation, whatever it may be. What we learn from history is not the story of such progress or evolution. Instead, we learn about multiple choices in manifold situations.

Given this presupposition, I should claim that what one sees in the story of baptism, confirmation, and the catechumenate is not necessarily progress from the baptism of adults to baptism of infants, from confirmation as an aspect of baptism to confirmation as something distinct, and from widespread catechetical instruction to its virtual eclipse. What one sees is not progress but change, brought about as the church responded to various kinds of occasions. This is my main thesis and it implies, I believe, that under circumstances changed still further the church must consider itself free to make further modifications, whether or not they have precedents in the past. I shall nonetheless argue that quite a few precedents exist.

The thesis can be broken down into three main subjects: baptism and infant baptism, confirmation, and the catechumenate.

Baptism and Infant Baptism

The debate between Joachim Jeremias and Kurt Aland[1] has lasted for about fifteen years now, and perhaps that is long enough. The main arena is New Testament exegesis, but practical theology or even liturgiology is also involved. The view of Jeremias put schematically is that New Testament Christians baptized infants and therefore we should baptize infants. Aland's view is that New Testament Christians did not baptize infants but we should nonetheless baptize infants. Then one should mention the position of Karl Barth: New Testament Christians did not baptize infants consequently we should not baptize infants. The only logical possibility remaining is that New Testament Christians baptized infants and therefore we should not baptize infants. But this is rather absurd.

Most of the second-century evidence, such as it is, casts little light on the question of infant baptism. The apologist Aristides, who probably wrote around 140, seems to avoid discussing baptism. He tells us that converts obtain forgiveness for past sins when they praise God and acknowledge that they have sinned because of ignorance.[2] If this statement implies baptism, such a baptism must be for persons beyond infancy. Again, Aristides writes that Christians praise God when a child is born to them; if it should happen to die young they give even more praise, on the ground that it passed through the world without sin.[3] Evidently Aristides and the other Christians he knew held no doctrine of original sin nor, more particularly, original guilt. It seems there was no special reason for infant baptism.[4]

Writing perhaps a decade later, the Roman apologist Justin describes at least the elements of baptism.

> Those who are convinced and believe that what we teach and say is true, and profess that they will be able to live in accordance with it—those persons are baptized.[5]

Justin's mention of a truth-criterion suggests that some philosophical theology, however elementary, was taught before baptism. His reference to living in accordance with the teaching implies the existence of some elementary moral instruction, perhaps of the sort found in his *Apology* itself. The implication of both these points is that baptism was normally for adults. This seems to be confirmed by his own explanation of baptism, which he claims has come down to him from the apostles.

> Since at our first birth we were born in ignorance and by necessity . . . and came to life in evil customs and wicked ways

> [the second birth takes place] so that we do not remain
> children of necessity or ignorance but [become children] of
> free will and knowledge and obtain remission of the sins we
> committed . . .[6]

This kind of expression, "children of" some abstraction, is a
Hebraism. Justin's use of it makes his statement unnecessarily
obscure. What he is trying to say is that in baptism the Christian
attaches himself to, or exercises, his free will and knowledge.
Elsewhere Justin says that in baptism the Christian receives the
Holy Spirit.[7] But to exercise free will and knowledge implies that
one is not an infant.

Similarly, around 180 when Theophilus of Antioch speaks of
baptism for those who are obtaining repentance and the remission
of sins through water,[8] it is most unlikely that he has infant
baptism in mind. In his view, infants are simple and sincere[9] : why
then baptize them?

In the early years of the third century, we encounter more
reliable evidence in Tertullian at Carthage. He gives us a basic
description of the baptismal rite in his treatise, *De corona*[10] :

> In the church under the hand of the president we declare that
> we renounce the devil, his pomp, and his angels. Then we are
> immersed thrice, giving somewhat fuller responses than what
> the Lord set forth in the gospel.

Other treatises reveal that baptism produces the remission of sins,
the restoration of the lost likeness of God, and the gift of the Holy
Spirit. One might suppose that a rite so heavily fraught with
significance would not be offered to infants. Therefore it is not
surprising to hear Tertullian stating that delay in baptism is advan-
tageous: why endanger sponsors, for one thing? To be sure, the
Lord said not to keep children from coming to him. But they
should come as adolescents, as students, as capable of being
taught. They should become Christians when they are capable of
knowing Christ. "Why," he inquires, "should the age of innocence
hasten to remission of sins?"[11] We might wonder what Tertullian
means by the age of innocence (*innocens aetas*), were it not that in
his treatise *Adversus Marcionem* he explicitly tells us, *parvuli,*
"infants," belong to the *innocens aetas,* whereas *pueri,* or "boys,"
are capable of judgment and blame. In Tertullian's view, at least as
he writes on baptism, the infant is incapable of judgment, is not

liable for its faults, and stands in no need of baptism for the remission of sins. In other writings he occasionally speaks of an infection or grime inherited from Adam, but his thought on the subject is not clear enough to ascribe a definite doctrine of original guilt to him, especially in view of his definite statements when writing on baptism.

To summarize matters thus far: in the age of the apologists there is no evidence for infant baptism, but there is, on the contrary, some striking evidence to show that only adults were baptized.

The *Apostolic Tradition* of Hippolytus shows us that at Rome in the early third century, possibly in the late second century as well, there was a mixed situation. It appears that the candidates for Christian initiation were definitely not infants, and that before entering upon instruction they were examined concerning the reasons for their conversion. The course normally lasted for three years, though it could be accelerated because of an individual's progress in faith and morals. After this they were baptized.

There was also the situation of "little children," described thus:

> They shall baptize the little children first. And if they can answer for themselves, let them answer. But if they cannot, let their parents answer or someone from their family.[12]

Evidently, then, there were two developments in baptismal practice. On the one hand, adult baptism had been combined with an extended period of instruction, longer than what we could infer from the *Didache* and Justin. On the other hand, the practice of child baptism had arisen along with adult baptism. Apparently this baptism was as a rule for children rather than for infants, although infants seem not to have been excluded. The baptismal rite involved exorcism, immersion, several unctions, and consignation. The bishop's prayer indicates the meaning of the rite:

> O Lord God, who didst count these persons worthy of the forgiveness of sins by the washing of regeneration, make them worthy to be filled with thy Holy Spirit and send thy grace upon them that they may serve thee . . .[13]

The vocabulary, already found in the New Testament, does not suggest that theological reflection had brought about the practice of baptizing children. To judge from the general tone of the

Apostolic Tradition, the practice more probably arose because of the Christian emphasis on family solidarity.

Even if Hippolytus did not write this treatise—a matter still *sub judice*—it almost certainly reflects the situation in some major church very early in the third century. Therefore the work is an important witness both to Christain usage at a time when both adults and children were being baptized, and to the rise and development of the catechumenate.

The slightly later testimony of Origen is important because it seems to show the *lex credendi* following the *lex orandi.* Three passages in his works, written at Caesarea in Palestine after 231, set forth Origen's view of infant baptism. He is aware that baptism is chiefly for the remission of sins. Since this is so, he argues, a problem arises. Why are little children (παιδια) baptized? When did they sin? Foregoing a treatment of his own speculative theology, it is sufficient to note that Origen contents himself with citing Job 14:4 from the Septuagint: "No one is free from uncleanness." This, he concludes, is the reason why little children are baptized. In another treatise he ascribes the practice to church observance, while in still another he adds that the tradition comes from the apostles.[14] He does not, however, seem to have heard of it during the years he spent at Alexandria. The idea of using Job 14:4 in support of universal sinfulness had earlier been expressed at Alexandria only by the Gnostic teacher Basilides.[15]

A more highly elaborated explanation was given at Carthage in 253, when Cyprian states that baptism ought not to be forbidden an infant,

> who being newly born has committed no sin, save that being carnally born according to Adam he has by his first birth contracted the infection of the ancient death. And indeed an infant approaches to receive the remission of sins more easily through this very fact, that the sins which are remitted unto him (in baptism) are not his own but another's.[16]

Cyprian insisted upon baptism on the second or third day after birth, in opposition to those who held the view that baptism was analogous to circumcision and should take place on the eighth day. It does not seem to have occurred to either side that the practice of infant baptism may have been related to the virtual collapse of the Carthaginian church during the persecution under

Decius. But whatever the cause of their defection there were obviously too many non-committed Christians.

From the fourth century we possess less information about baptism than we would wish. On the one hand, occasional statements made in passing suggest that infant baptism was becoming normative. Obviously it would be more common among children of Christians than among children of pagans![17] On the other hand, many Christians, even those brought up by Christian parents, deferred their baptism until the age of twenty-five or even thirty-five. It is hard to believe that they were simply following the pattern set by Constantine, who was baptized on his deathbed. There must have been a well established belief in the superiority of adult baptism to that of children. Certainly the achievements of many great fourth-century bishops suggest that deferred baptism did the people no harm, especially if it were combined with catechetical instruction. In addition, descriptions of the rites at Jerusalem show that adult baptism had remained normal there. Around this same time Gregory of Nyssa wrote *Against those who defer baptism,*[18] but his *Catechetical oration*[19] could have been neither comprehensible to children nor useful to catechists of children. Gregory of Nazianzus, writing in 381, expressed a compromise view. If infants run the risk of death, they should be baptized: "It is better to be consecrated without knowing it than to depart unsealed and uninitiated."[20] However, there is no reason to baptize other children until they are about three years old, that is, at an age when they can at least listen to Christian teaching and make responses on their own.

But during the fifth and sixth centuries infant baptism triumphed completely, possibly due in part to the barbarian invasions which gave impetus to anything that might promote the solidarity of social groups. At the same time, obviously, the catechumenate went under a cloud.

Confirmation

I shall not attempt to enter into the whole complicated question of the origins and development of confirmation, but it seems necessary to make a few statements about it. In its developed form in the West, confirmation was regarded as conveying the Holy Spirit by laying on the hands and was thus analogous to chrismation in the East. The situation was originally much more obscure, especially in the book of Acts to which later theologians appealed. From Acts one can prove almost anything. Either baptism effects the gift of the Spirit[21] or the Spirit is given before baptism. [22] One encounters either the sequence baptism-imposition-gift of the Spirit[23] or the sequence imposition-Spirit-baptism.[24] Finally, the Spirit's work is separate from the imposition of hands.[25] One of the points solidly established by G. W. H. Lampe is the extent to which later fathers picked and chose among these passages.[26] One can regard Tertullian's discussion in his treatise *On Baptism* as at least partly an attempt to clear up the confusing New Testament picture. He describes three stages of baptism: baptism proper, involving purification in water; unction, involving ordination to priesthood (of believers); and the imposition of hands, conferring the Holy Spirit.[27] What Tertullian is describing is three parts of *one* rite of initiation, not three rites. It was only around the time of the rebaptism controversy, which reached its height between 255 and 257, that in Rome Cornelius could differentiate deathbed baptism from "the sealing by the bishop" or, in Africa, Cyprian could get similar results from a different approach. [28] Although subsequently confirmation or chrismation did tend to get separated from baptism, there was still variety. From the late fourth-century Syrian document, *Apostolic Constitutions,* we read that Christian baptism requires chrism and the imposition of hands[29] and yet elsewhere in the same document we read that water is sufficient without oil or unguent.[30]

In the fifth century and early in the sixth there are significant statements about chrismation and confirmation which indicate that while the Spirit was received at baptism, its work continued and was indeed augmented as the Christian's life went on.[31]

It was necessary to say so much in order to see what connections could be made between infant baptism and the order of catechumens. It seems significant that as infant baptism grew and spread a tendency to split baptism into parts also occurred. In the course of this development, baptism would be conferred on infants where confirmation would be reserved for older children or for adults. Like infant baptism itself, the situation is related to the rapid growth of the churches. The Cornelius who insisted on "the sealing by the bishop" is the same man who quoted figures about the clergy and the widows of the Roman church in his concern for the life and growth of that church.[32] It was necessary to keep some control over the life of a growing institution.

In addition, one might expect that the separation of baptism and confirmation might have led to the introduction of a system of religious education for young people. Such however was not the case. The catechetical lectures of the fourth and fifth centuries are definitely for adults. In the light of this fact as well as of the paucity of our evidence for fourth-century infant baptism, it would be best to conclude that infant baptism did not really triumph until the fifth and sixth centuries.[33] When infant baptism triumphed, and when the separate rite of confirmation became widespread, the old catechetical system gradually disappeared not to be revived until the Reformation.

Development of the Christian Catechumenate

As one would expect, the catechumenate represents the formalization of something that existed informally from a very early time in the history of the church. According to Archbishop Carrington there was a rather simple catechism, Jewish in origin, underlying some of the New Testament epistles; other scholars too have seen this to be the case.[34] The more fully developed form of catechism is to be found in the *Didache* or "Teaching of the Twelve Apostles," which differentiates the way of life from the way of death, probably with an allusion to Deuteronomy. The "two ways" idea, and most of the content as well, is in origin thoroughly Jewish, or at least Jewish Christian. The same "two ways" are found in the *Epistle of Barnabas.* Probably a common Jewish source underlies both documents.[35]

The way of life begins thus: "First you shall love the God who made you, second, your neighbor as yourself; and whatever you do not wish done to yourself, do not do to another."[36] Then follows what looks like a later explanation of the moral commands with quotations from the Sermon on the Mount. Probably these quotations reflect a time when a Jewish catechism for proselytes was being Christianized. The author goes on to "the second commandment of the teaching," an expanded version of the second half of the decalogue. Later he warns us to avoid the first steps that lead to murder, adultery, idolatry, theft, and blasphemy, sins also listed in the decalogue. The "way of life" comes to an end with rather miscellaneous advice. The "way of death" consists of a long list of sins and sinners similar to those found in the Pauline epistles.

One remarkable feature about the "two ways" is the extreme practicality expressed in it. "Let your alms sweat into your hands until you know to whom you are giving."[37] At the end of the document we are told that "if you can bear the whole yoke of the Lord you will be perfect, but if you cannot, do what you can."[38] Even in the Sermon on the Mount passage we find this attitude: "If anyone takes what is yours from you, do not ask for it back; for you cannot do anything."[39] Probably this is good advice to give to children, but the candidates for baptism in the Didache are not children. Some have sons and daughters, others have slaves or servant-girls, still others are slaves themselves. The counsel is not cynical but realistic, even harshly so, for the Didachist expected it to be put into practice.

It should be added that whether or not the "two ways" was complete for the community for which it was written, the Didache does not present a full picture of Christian teaching. Anyone who approached Christian baptism with no more than the lesson of the "two ways" could hardly become a Christian. He was going to be baptized "in the name of the Father and the Son and the Holy Spirit." Accordingly, there must have been theological teaching at least up to the level implied by the eucharistic prayers of the treatise.

A few years after Didache and Barnabas were written, we find Ignatius of Antioch stating that baptisms are to take place only with the bishop's approval.[40] Since we assume that he was not just interested in getting his friends baptized, we infer that the bishop was to inquire into the way of life observed by the candidates, and in view of Ignatius' own concern with doctrine, also with what they had been taught. Unfortunately he tells us nothing about the precise content of the catechetical teaching. We can conclude, however, that at Antioch the content was close to his own theology.[41]

In the mid-second century, as we have already noted, the apologist Justin shows us that at Rome there was both systematic and moral catechetical teaching. When we reach the end of this century, we find two significant examples of catechetical teaching. One of these comes from Lyons, the *Demonstration of the Apostolic Preaching* by Irenaeus.[42] Based on "the three heads of our seal," God the Father, the Logos-Son, and the Holy Spirit, the treatise contains a history-of-salvation approach to theology and briefly retells the cardinal events of the Bible narrative, drawing out some of their most important theological implications. The exegetical method used is typology, and the results are familiar to anyone who has looked at the more extensive discussion in Irenacus' major work against heresies. Though the work is preserved only in Armenian, it is a summary of a kind of teaching that deeply influenced all Christian thinking. Writing in 1939, F. C. Burkitt said of the *Demonstration* that "apart from a few curiosities of expression . . . it sounds commonplace nowadays, but that is chiefly because the main lines of Christian theology and of Biblical interpretation followed the same course down to a hundred years ago . . . "[43]

The other witness to mid-second-century catechetical teaching is not a book in itself but can be recovered from the three books *To Autolycus* by Theophilus, bishop of Antioch. If we take what the Spanish pilgrim Egeria says about the first five weeks of catechism at Jerusalem in the fourth century, we find that all the elements in it are also present in the books of Theophilus. Egeria mentions literal and spiritual exegesis of all the scriptures, beginning with Genesis, as well as instruction on the resurrection and on faith. Theophilus deals with the exegesis of Genesis in his second book *To Autolycus*,[44] stating that the first two verses of Genesis contain the "primary" teachings of the divine scripture.[45] Later he shows how the law and the prophets offer consistent moral teaching[46] and, in the third book, how the law and the prophets agree with the gospels and other Christian books.[47] The first book deals with the doctrine of God,[48] includes a seemingly liturgical account of God's creative work,[49] and ends with discussions of resurrection and faith.[50] Along the way Theophilus says, "We are called Christians just because we are anointed with the oil of God."[51] Lampe suggests that the unction is metaphorical,[52] but in the light of the Jerusalem parallels it seems to be more. Indeed, one should add the passage from Cyril of Jerusalem which Lampe cites: it is chrismation which makes Christians Christian.[53] At the same time Eusebius is able to use the word 'chrism' for "the entire complex rite comprising Baptism as well as chrismation."[54]

Our main concern is not with chrismation or baptism, but with the probability that in the definitely theological passages of Theophilus' apologetic work we encounter an underlying structure which looks back to the bishop's own catechetical instructions. This suggests that the starting point of his theology is to be found within the life of the Christian community and in his responsibility as a catechist. It further implies that philosophical and theological questions were raised within the community; Christians did not need to wait for outsiders to bring them to their attention. In the catechetical school, at least at Antioch, a Christian culture was coming into existence in the second century.

A danger that often arises if one speaks of "Christian culture" is that we think of something timeless, eternal, not contemporary, and not very interesting. Such is not the case. The Genesis exegesis of Theophilus consists chiefly of efforts to solve problems raised by Jewish exegetes, by older Christians, and by Marcionite heretics. His attempts to hold the Old and New Testaments together are related to the separation proposed by Marcionites and other Gnostics. Theophilus' catechetical teaching, therefore, was contemporary in intention: he was dealing with the problems of his own time.

In addition, Theophilus states that, like other apologists, he became a Christian by reading the Old Testament. It is impossible, however, to believe that anyone ever became a Christian simply by reading the Old Testament. Such a reading must have been directed, presumably before baptism. The director would explain the relevance of Old Testament morality and the meaning of the passages in which Christ and the church were predicted or prefigured. In other words, the apologists were often trained by catechists; we may suppose that they in turn became catechists themselves.[55]

At Alexandria, as we might expect, the situation was rather complicated. We have not the vaguest idea about the teaching of Demetrius, bishop there from about 189 to about 232. All we know is that in his early years, there was a private school of

Christian higher education conducted by Clement, and that its lessons are enshrined, and partly concealed, in Clement's writings. A fragment entitled *Exhortation to endurance,* or *To the newly baptized* gives a simple summary, close to the slightly more advanced *Paedagogus.* The advice to "be modest toward women" and to "endure as a gentle and highminded man" suggests that adult males were being baptized. More important is the fact that out of this private school there emerged a trilogy, beginning with the *Protrepticus,* an appeal for pagans to be converted, continuing with the *Paedagogus,* mostly moral instruction (and often based on the Stoic Musonius Rufus), and ending with the *Stromata,* exercises in higher learning and counsels of perfection. With this atmosphere present in Alexandrian Christianity, it is small wonder that Origen could compare eternal life with an eternal school.

Origen himself was head of the church school at Alexandria from about 202 to 231. He was appointed to this position, and ultimately removed from it, by the bishop Demetrius. At an early age, and as a layman, he was instructing adult catechumens, some of whom became martyrs. Eusebius' notice of their deaths casts light on the school: one was still a catechumen; another, recently baptized; a third, still under instruction.[56]

Christian education at Alexandria seems to have been highly diversified. Clement took students through more elementary teaching in his *Paedagogus* before bringing them to the higher levels of the *Stromata,* and he seems to have done this work on his own as a private lay teacher. While in charge of catechetical teaching, Origen developed for the Alexandrian bishop a complete educational curriculum and he produced his major theological writings in relation to it. Later, at Caesarea, his teaching marked simply a development of what he had taught earlier. There are two points to be noted in this flowering of Christian culture at Alexandria: (1) the diversity and freedom of speculation, as long as what was generally regarded as heresy was avoided; (2) the closeness of the relation between the educational process and the productivity of the theologians.

Our picture of the kind of teaching that went on in the church school at Alexandria is rather fragmentary, especially since our main informant, Eusebius, was defending Origen against various accusations and not setting forth a clear description. We learn, too, that as in most schools, the instruction was graded. Eusebius speaks of Heraclas, who later became bishop, as teaching "introduction" to beginners, while Origen himself taught the more advanced students. Apparently, the school provided instruction in grammar and rhetoric, geometry and arithmetic, before the courses in philosophy and theology began. We should, however, beware of assuming that the courses were simply intellectual. Speculative theology came at the end of the curriculum not the beginning, and the pattern of introductory scripture reading thus set by Origen lasted for more than a century.

This pattern is mentioned in his rather late *Homilies on Numbers,* where he contrasts the clarity of the books of Esther, Judith, Tobit, and Wisdom with the obscurity of Leviticus, and the clarity of the gospels, the Apostle, and the psalms with the mysteries of Numbers. Beginners were to read the clear books not the obscure ones.[57] We find a very similar pattern in Athanasius' *Paschal Letter* for the year 367. He recommends to the catechumens the Wisdom of Solomon and the Wisdom of Sirach and Esther and Judith and Tobit, adding the so-called *Didache of the Apostles* and the *Shepherd* of Hermas).[58]

Among Jewish teachers there were also recommendations to postpone discussion of the more obscure passages of scripture, such as the visions of Ezekiel, the poetry of the Song of Songs, or the opening chapters of Genesis. It is, therefore, rather surprising to find an Oxyrhynchus papyrus with a note of introduction for a catechumen "being instructed in Genesis."[59] Were his teachers aware of the pitfalls? Did they keep him away from Origen's commentary?

In general, Christians seem to have believed that the gains outweighed the risks. Irenaeus paraphrased the creation story in his *Demonstration of the Apostolic Preaching* while Theophilus, as we have seen, devoted much of his second book *To Autolycus* to Genesis, providing long quotations, exegesis, and paraphrases. It was natural, therefore, for Eusebius to refer to Theophilus' books as "elementary." He meant by this that like other works by Theophilus they were suitable for use in catechetical teaching.[60] So we find that in later times catechesis took the form of lectures on all the scriptures, beginning with Genesis. Two examples are Cyril of Jerusalem and Augustine.

In fourth-century Jerusalem, to judge from the eighteen catechetical lectures of the bishop Cyril, the teaching given catechumens was fairly simple and straightforward, even though it was
completed with further mystical lectures on the sacraments. The
lectures followed the outline given by the creed and ended on
Palm Sunday. We cannot be sure, however, that in all churches the
catechumens were equally well taught. It was a privilege for
Christians to visit the city and, especially, to be baptized there. [61]
Gregory of Nazianzus warns rich converts against saying, "A
bishop must baptize me, preferably a metropolitan, and, for that
matter, the bishop of Jerusalem." He insists that grace depends
not on places but on the Spirit.[62] When we read the travel diary
of Egeria, therefore, we must bear in mind that she is a tourist
noting what was unique and colorful in Jerusalem, not what was
being done everywhere.[63]

At Jerusalem, the preparations for baptism were elaborate. On
the eve of the first Sunday in Lent the candidates for baptism
(competentes) separated themselves from the catechumens as a
whole and handed in their names. That Sunday the bishop inter-
rogated the neighbors of the competentes to find out if they were
of blameless moral character. If they were not, their candidacy
was put off. Every morning in Lent, from the first hour through
the third, the bishop gave literal and spiritual exegesis of "all the
scriptures"; he also gave teaching about the resurrection and about
faith.

As at Alexandria in the late second and early third centuries
catechetical theology had tended to develop into higher Christian
education, so now under the lead of Gregory of Nyssa, an admirer
of Origen, a similar move was made. Gregory's Oratio catechetica
magna[64] was addressed not to the catechumens themselves but to
those who were teaching them and needed a systematic theology
based on metaphysics, not simply on scripture. Thus Gregory
devoted four chapters to the doctrine of one God in three persons,
twenty-eight chapters to the history of salvation in Christ from the
creation of man to redemption, and four chapters to the sacraments and their relation to faith. In the section on the history of
salvation, he occasionally indicated that according to the tradition
of the church various items contain deeper meanings. For example, the shape of the cross points to the all-embracing love of God.

Simpler instruction naturally continued to be given, and from Theodore of Mopsuestia we possess a *Liber ad baptizandos*[65] with ten homilies on the creed (for use before baptism) and six homilies on the Lord's Prayer, baptism, and eucharist (for use after baptism). We also possess the treatise *De mysteriis* by St. Ambrose, which shows that during Lent the bishop of Milan gave daily instruction on Christian morals and the elements of Christianity.[66] One can also add mention of Augustine's treatise *De catechizandis rudibus*.

In this essay we have seen something of the ways in which baptism and infant baptism, confirmation, and the catechumenate existed, with both fixity and modification, during the early centuries of the church's life. Changes seem to have taken place in relation to changing social conditions. The purpose remained the same: to present candidates for baptism who, in the words of I Peter 3:15, would "always be prepared to make a defense to any one who calls you to account for the hope that is in you."

Could the process of change have flowed in different directions? An examination of the rite called 'scrutiny,' which grew up alongside baptism in the fourth century, suggests that modifications could be made. In Rome and in Africa, scrutiny was a rite involving renunciation of the devil, performed with exorcisms and supplications. At the end of the fifth century, when the courtier Senarius wrote to John the Deacon at Rome and inquired about the meaning of scrutiny, John told him that it was an examination of a baptismal candidate in regard to scripture, salvation, and faith in God the Father. It was preceded by instruction and it obviously had theological-pedagogical significance.[67] Dondeyne, followed by Leclerq, pointed out that this significance was reinforced by John the Deacon, who it seems early in the sixth century became Pope John I.[68] There is thus some precedent, either in this instance or more generally in early church history, for the vitalization or revitalization of the catechumenate as a setting for creative Christian learning.

NOTES

1. J. Jeremias, *Die Kindertaufe in den ersten vier Jahrhunderten* (Göttingen: Vandenhoeck & Rupprecht, 1958); *Infant Baptism in the First Four Centuries*, trans. David Cairns (London: S.P.C.K., 1960); K. Aland, *Taufe und Kindertaufe. 40 Sätze sur Aussage des Neuen Testaments* (Gütersloh: Gütersloher Verlag, 1971); K. Aland, *Did the Early Church Baptize Infants*, trans. G. R. Beasley-Murray, Library of History and Doctrine (Philadelphia: Westminster Press, 1963); J. Jeremias, *Nochmals: Die Anfänge der Kindertaufe*, Theologische Existenz Huete 101 (Munich: Kaiser Verlag, 1962); J. Jeremias, *The Origins of Infant Baptism*, trans. Dorothea M. Barton, Studies in Historical Theology 1 (London: SCM Press, 1963).

2. Aristides, *Apol.* 17.4. See Migne, *PG* 5.

3. *Ibid.*, 15.11. See Migne, *PG* 5.

4. H. Windisch, *Taufe und Sünde im ältesten Christentum bis auf Origines* (Tübingen: Mohr, 1908): 383—384.

5. Justin, 1 *Apol.* 61—2. See Migne, *PG* 6.420.

6. *Ibid.*, 61.10. See Migne, *PG* 6.421.

7. Justin, *Dialogus* 29:1. See Migne, *PG* 6.537.

8. Theophilus, *Ad Autolycum* 2.16. trans. R. M. Grant (Oxford: Clarendon Press, 1970): 52—55.

9. *Ibid.*, 2.25. See Grant, pp. 66—69.

10. Tertullian, *De Corona* 3. See Migne, *PL* 2.70.

11. Tertullian, *De Baptismo* 18.4—5. See J. G. P. Borleffs (ed.) *Corpus Christianorum, Series Latina* 1 (Turnhout: Brepols, 1954).

12. See Bernard Botte (ed.), *La Tradition Apostolique de Saint Hippolyte. Essai de Reconstitution*, Liturgiewissenschaftliche Quellen und Forschungen 39 (Münster: Aschendorffsche Verlagsbuchhandlung, 1963): 21.4. For English translation, see G. Dix (ed. and trans.), *The Treatise on the Apostolic Tradition of St. Hippolytus of Rome*, 2nd ed. (London: S.P.C.K., 1968).

13. *Ibid.*, 22.1.

14. Origen, *Luc. hom.* 14; see Migne, *PG* 13.1833—1839. Origen, *Lev. hom.* 8.3; see Migne, *PG* 12, 494—496. Origen, *Rom. comm.* v.9; see Migne, *PG* 14.1043—1048.

15. Cf. Clement, *Stromata* IV, 1265—67. See Migne, *PG* 8.1292—1293; Contrast this with 1 Clem. 17.3—4. 1.244.

16. Cyprian, *Ep.* 64.2—6. See Migne, *PL* 4.389—393. Cf. N. P. Williams, *The Ideas of the Fall and of Original Sin* (London, Longmans-Green, 1927), 296.

17. J. C. Didier, "Le pedobaptisme au IVe siècle: documents nouveaux," *Melanges de science religieuse* 6 (1949): 233—246.

18. Migne, *PG* 46.416—431.

19. J. H. Srawley (ed.), *The Catechetical Oration of St. Gregory of Nyssa* (Cambridge: S.P.C.K., 1917).

20. Migne, *PG* 36.400A.

21. Acts 2:38.

22. Acts 10:44ff.

23. Acts 8:16ff; 19:5.

24. Acts 9:12, 17ff.

25. Acts 6:3ff; 13:2ff.
26. G. W. H. Lampe, *The Seal of the Spirit, A Study in the Doctrine of Baptism and Confirmation in the New Testament and the Fathers* (London: S.P.C.K., 1951).
27. Tertullian, *De Baptismo* 6–8. Cf. above, fn. 10.
28. Lampe, *Seal,* pp. 170–179.
29. *Apost. Const.* VII.44.3. See F. S. Funk (ed.), *Didascalia et Constitutiones Apostolorum* (Paderborn: Schoeningh, 1905): 450.
30. *Ibid.,* VII.22.3. Funk, p. 407. See also Lampe, *Seal,* p. 209.
31. See Lampe, *Seal,* 301–303.
32. Eusebius, *H.E.* VI.43.15 and 11. See Migne, *PG* 20. 615–630.
33. F. H. Kettler, "Taufe," *Die Religion in Geschichte und Gegenwart* 6, 3rd ed. (Tübingen: J. B. Mohr, 1962): 638.
34. P. Carrington, *The Primitive Christian Catechism* (Cambridge: University Press, 1940).
35. J. P. Audet (ed.), *La Didache. Instructions des Apôtres* (Paris: Gabalda, 1958). See also R. A. Kraft (trans.), *Barnabas and the Didache,* The Apostolic Fathers (New York: Nelson, 1965): 4–16.
36. *Didache,* p. 226. Kraft, *Barnabas,* p. 138.
37. *Ibid.,* 1.6.
38. *Ibid.,* 6.2.
39. *Ibid.,* 1.4.
40. Ignatius of Antioch, *Smyrn,* 8.2. See Migne, *PG* 5.852.
41. From *Trall* 5 we infer that it had lower and higher levels. See Migne, *PG* 5.781–783.
42. See Irenaeus, *Proof of the Apostolic Preaching,* ed. K. T. Mekerttschian and S. C. Wilson, Patrologia Orientalis, 5 (Paris: Firmin Didot, 1919).
43. F. C. Burkitt, *Pagan Philosophy and the Christian Church,* ed. S. A. Cook, F. E. Adcock, M. D. Charlesworth, N. H. Baynes, Cambridge Ancient History, 12 (Cambridge: University Press, 1939): 475.
44. Theophilus, *Ad Autolycum* II.10–31. Cf. Grant, pp. 38–81.
45. *Ibid.,* II.10. Grant, pp. 38–39.
46. *Ibid.,* II.34–35. Grant, pp. 82–84.
47. *Ibid.,* III.9–14. Grant, pp. 110–119.
48. *Ibid.,* I.1–5. Grant, pp. 2–9.
49. *Ibid.,* I.6–7. Grant, pp. 8–11.
50. *Ibid.,* I.8.13–14. Grant, pp. 10–13.
51. *Ibid.,* I.12. Grant, pp. 16–17.
52. Lampe, *Seal,* p. 114.
53. *Ibid.,* p. 219.
54. *Ibid.,* p. 213.
55. On this point in regard to Justin, cf. W. Bousset, *Jüdisch-hellenistischer Schulbetrieb in Alexandria und Rom,* Forschungen zur Religion und Literatur des Alten und Neuen Testaments 23 (Göttingen: Vandenhoeck and Ruprecht, 1915): 282–308.
56. Eusebius, *H.E.* VI.3–4. See Migne, *PG,* 20.525–532.
57. Origen, *Num. Hom.* 27.1. See Migne, *PG* 12:780. The *mandata Sapientiae* could refer to either Solomon or Sirach.
58. Athanasius, *Epist. pasch.* 39. See Migne, *PG* 26.1438. "Youths" are encouraged to learn "the wisdom of the polymath Sirach"; cf. *Apost. Const.*

VIII.47.85 (Funk, p. 592). Note also that Eusebius, *H.E.* III. 3.6. (cf. Migne, *PG* 20.215–220) refers to the *Shepherd* as "judged indispensable for those who need introductory instruction."

59. *P. Oxy.* XXXVI.2785.

60. Eusebius, *H.E.* IV.24. Migne, *PG.*20.389.

61. Migne, *PG* 33.331–1060. For English, see F. L. Cross (ed.), *St. Cyril of Jerusalem's Lectures on the Christian Sacraments* (London: S.P.C.K., 1951).

62. Migne, *PG* 36.396B.

63. Peregrinatio Egeriae, cf. H. Pétré (ed.), *Etherie: Journal de Voyage*, Sources Chrétiennes 21 (Paris: Editions du Cerf, 1948).

64. Gregory of Nyssa, *Oratio Catechetica Magna.* Cf. above, fn. 19.

65. Theodore of Mopsuestia, *Liber ad baptizandos.* Cf. A. Mingana (ed. and trans.), *Commentary of Theodore of Mopsuestia on the Lord's Prayer and on the Sacraments of Baptism and the Eucharist*, Woodbrooke Studies V–VI, (Cambridge: Heffer & Son, 1933).

66. Ambrose, *De Sacramentis, De Mysteriis*, ed. B. Botte, Sources Chrétiennes 25 bis (Paris: Editions due Cerf, 1961). As for the six sermons *De Sacramentis* ascribed to him, the researches of Klaus Gamber have again made it likely that the author was not Ambrose but Nicetas of Remesiana, on the Yugoslav-Bulgarian border. These sermons add nothing new since they seem to be based on Cyril of Jerusalem and Ambrose. Cf. K. Gamber, *Die Autorschaft von De Sakramentis*, Studia Patristica et Liturgica 1 (Regensburg: Pustet, 1967).

67. Johannes Diaconus, *Epistula ad Senarium.* See Migne, *PL* 59.399–408.

68. A. Dondeyne, "La discipline des scrutins dans l'Eglise latine avant Charlemagne," *Revue d'Histoire Ecclesiastique* 28 (1932): 5–33, 751–788.

CHAPTER III

Dissolution of the Rite of Christian Initiation

Nathan D. Mitchell

TO STUDY THE DISINTEGRATION OF A LITURGICAL RITE IS TO DO MORE THAN assess a ritual malfunction: it is to grow aware of a more fundamental decay within Christian life—a decay that resonates throughout Christian faith, catechesis, theology, and praxis. It is not so unusual for a ritual to break down. What is unusual, and instructive, is to discover why rituals are so mismanaged that they become grotesque and unrecognizable.

This essay will ask why so seminal a rite as Christian initiation disintegrated and finally collapsed into three separate and dislocated moments of water-baptism, confirmation, and eucharist. Attention will focus on the western church, in which the problem of dislocation was felt most acutely. The period under consideration spans roughly eight hundred years. It opens at the beginning of the sixth century, when we find relatively undisputed evidence for baptism at Rome in the famous letter of John the Deacon to the Roman nobleman Senarius.[1] The period closes with the full development of a scholastic theology of initiation by Thomas Aquinas (1225–1274).

The scope of this paper does not permit a thorough liturgical chronicle of all the events which led to the demise of a unified rite of Christian initiation in the West. Such a chronicle would need to begin with early fragments of evidence from sources such as the *Didache*, or Justin Martyr, or from a reconstructed text such as the *Apostolic Tradition* of Hippolytus, with its fully developed, fully integrated ritual of prebaptismal anointing, triple immersion in water, postbaptismal anointings, and baptismal eucharist.[2] One would then need to trace the impact of a source such as that of Hippolytus throughout a wide variety of churches, and to ask how

50

that rite compared with other local, indigenous usages. In short, a complete inventory of the way Christian initiation was fractured and torn apart in the West would necessitate several volumes of comparative liturgics.

Because completeness is neither possible nor desirable here, we shall have to be content with selecting examples that illustrate some of the problems Christian communities faced in their efforts to incorporate new members through baptismal regeneration. My remarks will thus fall into the following three areas: A *"pre-history" of the decline of initiation in the medieval West.* Here I shall attempt to select examples that reflect, at least partially, the evolution and breakdown of initiation practice as it affected some of the principal liturgical families in the West; *Aquinas and the scholastic standardization of initiation theology.* Because the wide dissemination of Aquinas' thought has colored our theology of confirmation down to the present day, some understanding of the Thomist position is essential; *A consideration of some of the reasons why the western church found it impossible to maintain the integrity of Christian initiation.* These reasons vary widely, but they include such factors as shifts in church structure, the declining intelligibility of symbols, and the failure to understand the relation between memorial (*anamnesis*) and invocation (*epiclesis*) in the sacraments.

One final point of clarification: the term 'initiation' is used comprehensively in this paper to embrace all those acts by which Christians are *made* (for Christians are indeed made, not born). These include preliminary rites (exorcisms, exsufflations, anointings, and signings); the act of immersion into water (together with the profession of faith); the post-baptismal ceremonies (anointings, consignation, imposition of hands, etc.); and the baptismal eucharist. When I refer to the breakdown or disintegration of initiation, I have in mind the dismemberment of the ritual elements just outlined into distinct sacramental moments separated by intervals of time (represented, for example, by the tendency to delay eucharistic communion until the "age of reason" or the "age of discretion").

The historico-liturgical understanding of the changing contours of Christian initiation has been advanced considerably since the mid-1960's by the publication of two important works: Canon J. D. C. Fisher's *Christian Initiation: Baptism in the Medieval West,* and Father Leonel Mitchell's *Baptismal Anointing.*[3] Both these studies are extraordinarily valuable in tracing the historical fortunes of the rites of initiation. Since Fisher's book already gives us a fairly comprehensive account of how initiation fared in the medieval West, I shall not reproduce his findings here in any detail. However it may prove useful to outline some of the conclusions reached by Canon Fisher; to discuss some of the factors that contributed to the demise of a unified rite of initiation such as one finds in earlier texts like the *Apostolic Tradition,* as well as to ask what factors promoted the emergence of a rite of episcopal confirmation viewed as having effects theologically distinct from those of baptism. I think it can be safely argued that, in the case of episcopal confirmation, the rite emerges first and the theological constructions follow later.

In dealing with Christian initiation during the period 500–1274, the most obvious problem is also the one most difficult to resolve satisfactorily: why does the West eventually elect to maintain the episcopal presidency of a portion of the initiation rite, *viz.,* the laying on of hands and consignation with chrism, at the expense of the very unity of the rite itself? Moreover, why does the eucharist, as the act which consummates baptismal incorporation and sealing, get separated and delayed?[4] We know, of course, that the growing practice of infant baptism had something to do with the delay in eucharistic participation. We know, too, that the Christian East resolved the matter quite differently, maintaining the unity of the total initiation rite at the expense of episcopal presidency, and continuing to baptize, confirm, and communicate candidates in a single rite, even in the case of infants.

Certainly, one can argue that the West does not present a unified front on these issues during this period. One can point to evidence that the situation in Rome itself, where several baptisteries existed at an early period,[5] was different from the situation in Northern Italy, in Spain, in Gaul, or in the German territories. Indeed, one could defend the thesis that throughout this entire period there exists no single western rite of initiation, but rather a collection of local rites similar in structure yet divergent in significant details. Furthermore, these local rites were themselves subject to such a degree of evolution that general assertions about "Roman" or "Gallican" or "old Spanish" rites always need to be nuanced by specific details about particular places at particular times.

Initiation rites did not cease their evolution with the death of the last Church Father. Throughout the time under consideration here, such rites continued to develop and fluctuate. A brief glance at some of the North Italian liturgical traditions will illustrate this point. Writing from fourth century Milan, Ambrose describes, in his *De Mysteriis,* a "spiritual seal" (*spiritale signaculum*) which followed the neophyte's clothing with a white robe.[6] This seal seems to have consisted of the sign of the cross made by the bishop on the neophyte's forehead and it may have included the use of oil.[7] Unquestionably, Ambrose associated this seal with reception of the sevenfold gift of the Holy Spirit; for him it gives the Christian participation in the same Spirit that had anointed Jesus for his work and mission.

Yet despite the importance Ambrose attached to this seal or the prestige of the church of Milan, use of the *signaculum* did not become universal in North Italian churches. Evidence in fact points either to its disappearance or, at a somewhat later date, to a confusion between the old Ambrosian seal and the act of post-baptismal anointing.[8]

Other elements within the cluster of initiation rites suffered similar disappearances or dislocations. For instance, the eighth century rite of Aquileia, known to us from a letter of Bishop Maxentius to Charlemagne, appears to have neither an episcopal imposition of hands nor a second postbaptismal anointing.[9] Even Milan itself seems to have temporarily dropped the episcopal imposition of hands. That such was the case is implied in a description of baptism sent to Charlemagne by Odilbert, bishop from 805 to 813. In that letter, the bishop is said to impose hands on the neophyte only at the end of the eucharist, *after* communion.[10] Fisher suggests that Odilbert has simply attached the laying on of hands to the end of his ritual in an effort to comply with Roman practice, and thus to please the reform-minded Charlemagne.[11] One can infer that, for some time prior to this Carolingian pressure, the Milanese church had considered baptism, unction, and eucharist as an integral rite, complete and sufficient without any additional imposition of hands by the bishop. This inference is supported further by the ninth century *Sacramentary of Biasca,* where the episcopal laying on of hands had once more been discontinued.[12] Thus one gathers that Carolingian efforts at reforming baptism met with very impermanent success in North Italian churches.

Similar illustrations could be drawn from the practice of Gallican and Spanish communities. But my intention here is simply to indicate that the practices associated with Christian initiation fluctuated throughout the West during this period. The impact of such local variability needs to be kept strongly in mind whenever one speaks about baptism in the medieval West.

Granting such local variation, one is still able to make an educated appraisal of the way western Christians were initiated in the time between 500 and 1274 A.D. I will here summarize some of the things we *do* know.

There is reason to believe that in Rome itself the primitive unity of Christian initiation was by and large substantially preserved until at least the twelfth century.[13] It should be obvious that not all candidates for baptism in Rome were personally baptized by the bishop of Rome, nor were all those candidates between the sixth and twelfth centuries adults. The letter of John the Deacon to Senarius recognizes that neophytes were often, quite literally, babies.[14] Nor should one forget about those extraordinary cases like the baptism of persons in danger of death or the complicated question of those who had previously undergone baptism by heretics. Such non-normative situations are clearly not covered by the preceding assertion.

In spite of many exceptions, however, one can say that for an appreciable span of time Rome itself sought to maintain Christian initiation as a single ritual unit under the presidency of the bishop. The assumption is that at Rome, until the twelfth century, the ceremonies following the immersion in water continued to include both the two postbaptismal anointings found already in Hippolytus' third century rite (that is, an anointing of the neophyte's head by the presbyter, followed by a second anointing by the bishop), and eucharistic communion.[15] Fisher thinks that outside the pope's own church, the second postbaptismal anointing was performed by suffragan bishops.[16] Such a state of affairs is plausible, even if not indisputable.

Outside Rome the situation between the sixth and twelfth centuries is murky. The Gallican arrangement can serve as an illustration, being characteristically confusing. Judging from late fifth century evidence, as we have it from Gennadius of Marseilles, some parts of Gaul did include such post-baptismal ceremonies as the episcopal laying on of hands and anointing with chrism. [17] These elements later appear to have dropped out of use, in much the same way that Ambrose's *spiritale signaculum* disappeared from the Milanese and North Italian rites. It may be that the Gallican churches connected the bestowal of the Spirit with the postbaptismal anointing by the presbyter,[18] or perhaps the question of when and how the Spirit was given to Christians was simply left ambiguous.

In any case, Charlemagne's endeavors at reform give us some clue about Gallican initiation in the late eighth and early ninth centuries. Charlemagne insisted on two items of reform:[19] one dealing with infant baptism and the other with the case of adults. In both cases however the *times* of baptism were to be restricted to the classical period of Easter and Pentecost, except *in articulo mortis*. This would permit more infants to be baptized in a rite at which the local bishop could preside. Moreover, provision had to be made for the baptism of adult pagans brought into the empire as a result of Charlemagne's campaigns of imperial expansion. The most notable feature of the adult rite was an episcopal imposition of hands *after communion,* the same sort of addition we saw occuring in early ninth-century Milan under bishop Odilbert.[20]

Whatever the ritual success of Carolingian reforms in Gaul, their impact on subsequent theology was enormous. The ninth century writer Rabanus Maurus (+856 A.D.) developed a theological interpretation of the postbaptismal imposition of hands which was to have lasting repercussions. While he does not deny that the Spirit is associated with the presbyteral anointing of the neophyte's head after baptism, Rabanus argues that the episcopal imposition of hands and chrismation *confer* the Spirit.[21] This sort of language forces him to explain the difference between the two postbaptismal acts. His explanation sounds ominously familiar: the first anointing after baptism, done by the presbyter, effects the descent of the Spirit and the consecration of the Christian; the second anointing, the episcopal chrismation and laying on of hands, brings the grace of the Spirit into the baptized "with all the fulness of sanctity, knowledge and power."[22]

This kind of theological rationale is bolstered by the rite with which Rabanus was familiar. In that rite the postcommunion imposition of hands was not performed immediately after the Mass of the Paschal Vigil, but rather *a week later* on the Octave of Easter.[23] We should notice, then, what has happened: the pre-Carolingian rite in Gaul might have been content to say that full initiation has been accomplished by the presbyteral anointing of the neophyte's head, but under the pressure of reform, the episcopal imposition of hands and chrismation is added a week later. Fisher is probably right when he suggests that this represents another Gallican effort to supply whatever by Roman standards was lacking.[24] Rabanus offers a theological justification for what had become a ritual fact. Moreover, we can begin to see a time-wedge being inserted between the various parts of Christian baptism. Thus, by the early ninth century we are already well on the road to "confirmation," to a split in the ensemble of initiation rites, and to a style of theology that will legitimate them both. As a result, to write the story of the dissolution of Christian initiation is to write about the emergence of episcopal confirmation as a rite separated from baptism. These are some of the conclusions reached by Fisher's study.

Our second point centers around the factors which contributed both to the demise of a unified rite of initiation and to the emergence of a rite of episcopal confirmation. However, one should avoid assuming that confirmation is simply the product of Carolingian enthusiasm for reform. The history of worship is something like the human body: it has a way of giving off danger signals far in advance of the breakdown.

Despite the problems it presents for us today, episcopal confirmation was not an unwelcome bastard that appeared suddenly to embarrass the Christian pedigree. There were signals and symptoms of its eventual appearance much earlier in western liturgical history. Space does not permit a catalogue of all these symptoms, but mention of two of them will prove profitable.

Already in Cyprian's time, the middle of the third century, there existed some theological temporizing over how, where, and when the Spirit operates in the mysteries of baptism. Naturally, Cyprian affirms the presence and power of the Spirit in baptism; otherwise, how could the washing produce rebirth or the creation of a new, spiritual man?[25] But the bishop of Carthage fudges somewhat, for he also wants to point out that the Spirit is not "given" or "received" except through the laying on of hands.[26] The result is confusing, and Cyprian attempts to clarify the matter through a rather curious exegesis of the creation story. He remarks that baptism signifies Adam's formation from clay, while the reception of the Spirit through the imposition of hands signals the breathing into him of the Spirit of life.[27]

Austin Milner has suggested that Cyprian's exegesis is reminiscent of Irenaeus' view about two distinct functions of the Spirit in the church.[28] The Irenaean view runs as follows:[29] through a *formative* function the Spirit unites the church into a single body, much as water unites grains of flour, and dust particles congeal to form Adam's body; through a *nutritive* function the Spirit refreshes all Christians with a single drink and bestows on them the same anointing which Christ received from the Father. This sort of distinction seems to find resonance in Cyprian's attempt to understand the relation between baptismal washing and the imposition of hands. It is unclear, however, whether or not Irenaeus himself intended to relate his views about the Spirit's working in the church to any particular liturgical rite.[30]

The problem faced by Cyprian reveals that at a fairly early date there was some debate not only about when and how Christians received the gift of the Spirit, but also about the Spirit's relation to particular elements within the initiation rite. In some respects the theology of Rabanus Maurus simply continues that type of debate, but with this crucial difference: the ninth-century rite known to Rabanus had been reshaped, and a week's wedge had been driven between the baptismal washing and the episcopal imposition of hands. As time passes, that week's wedge will develop into an interval of several years, and a theology will be constructed to account for the difference in terms of exact sacramental effects.

There is another historical item which signals the ultimate

emergence of a separate, distinct rite of episcopal confirmation. The earlier emphasis on imposition of hands in Christian initiation is gradually displaced by emphasis on the symbolism of anointing with chrism. We have already noticed that in Ambrose there is a close connection between the *spiritale signaculum* and the seven-fold gifts of the Spirit. Whether or not Ambrose's seal involved the use of oil is open to debate. In any case, later Milanese documents like the twelfth-century order of Beroldus, tended to confuse the Ambrosian seal with a form of unction.[31]

Once again, this displaced emphasis on postbaptismal chrisma-tion by the bishop did not mushroom overnight. Already in Augustine there is a vocabulary that will prove very congenial to the speculations of later theologians, preoccupied as they were with the precise sacramental effects of chrismation in relation to baptismal washing. Speaking to neophytes, Augustine remarks:

> . . . you, too, in a certain sense were first ground by the lowly practice of fasting and by the sacred rite of exorcism. Next the water of baptism was added, by which, as it were, you were moistened in order to be formed into bread. But there is yet no bread without fire. What, then, does fire signify? Holy Chrism, the oil that supplies the fire, the sacrament of the Holy Spirit. . . . That is how the Holy Spirit comes, the sacrament of fire after the sacrament of water, and you are made a bread, namely, the body of Christ. And that is how unity is signi-fied.[32]

Certainly, such a text cannot be pressed too far. Augustine still knows Christian initiation as a unified rite, and his homiletic hyperbole cannot be taken for precise theological statement, espe-cially when read out of context. A later age will be less scrupulous about its use of Augustine. He is, it will be remembered, Aquinas' favorite patristic source. And Aquinas had, after all, no *Clavis Patrum* to help him distinguish which of Augustine's works were genuine and which were spurious. Whatever Augustine himself may have intended to say about post-baptismal chrismation, a later theology will find his vocabulary useful for defending a separate rite of confirmation.[33]

One could expand almost indefinitely the list of historical signals that point to the future dismemberment of Christian initia-tion into three distinct sacraments: baptism, confirmation, and eucharist. Here I have suggested only two of them. The list would have to include the controversies over the rebaptism of heretics, documents like the letter of Innocent I to bishop Decentius of Gubbio, conciliar and synodal legislation such as that from the Council of Orange (441 A.D.).[34] All these played a significant role in the rise of confirmation in the western church. For the moment, however, it is necessary to turn to the theology of Aquinas in order to see how this gradual liturgical evolution was given a scholastic armor.

In dealing with Aquinas, three questions will occupy our attention: what rite of Christian initiation did he know? how did he understand sacraments? and what did he think about the relation between baptism and confirmation?

Unfortunately, Aquinas never cites in full the rituals upon which he theologizes. Still we are not utterly lost for information. The *Summa Theologiae* permits us to piece together several details about thirteenth-century initiation as Thomas knew it.[35]

Besides the ordinary details about formulae of administration and the sort of chrism used, Aquinas does supply us with the following information.[36] 1) Easter and Pentecost are still recognized as the appropriate times for the administration of baptism and confirmation *solemniter*.[37] On at least some occasions the bishop was present and celebrated the rites of initiation integrally. 2) Presbyters are the ordinary ministers of baptism, while bishops are the usual presiders at confirmation.[38] 3) Aquinas admits that the *usus communis ecclesiae* tends in his time toward a separation between baptism and confirmation, with the latter normally reserved to bishops alone. 4) One reason why this split between baptism and confirmation had occurred was the large size of dioceses.[39] Thomas defends what is evidently becoming more and more the standard usage of the churches by a reference to the governance of the Holy Spirit. This is important because it means that as far as Aquinas is concerned, the concrete practice of the church becomes, at any given period of time, a justifiable norm of sacramental propriety. Thus the rite of confirmation is, in his view, an indication that the church follows the *sapientiam Christi*.[40]

I suspect there is a hidden agenda in Thomas' argument. It is quite conceivable that he finds himself having to defend liturgical practices that are still considered novel in some churches. After all, not all Thomas' opponents were straw men designed for rapid demolition by syllogistic argument. Some of them were real flesh and blood opponents. And if we are to believe Michel Andrieu, some churches in the thirteenth century still preserved the more ancient custom of baptizing, confirming, and communicating infants in one single act of initiation.[41] Thus Aquinas may have felt it necessary to defend a more recent liturgical innovation against adherents of an older discipline.

To what sort of liturgical books would Aquinas have had access? One is tempted to believe that he would have known some version of the *Roman Pontifical*. The term 'pontifical,' however, is not earlier than the end of the thirteenth or beginning of the fourteenth century.[42] Earlier terms used for what eventually became the 'pontifical' included *Ordo* (as in the *Ordines Romani*), *Ordinarium papale* or *Ordinarium domni papae* (a term used in the thirteenth century) and *Liber pontificalis* (which often replaced terms like *Ordo* or *Ordinarium* in the fourteenth century).[43] Despite these problems of terminology, however, documents that represent the liturgical genre known subsequently as 'pontificals' were indeed known three or four centuries before Aquinas' time.[44] Moreover, with the increasing prominence of such pontificals in the tenth and eleventh centuries, the sacramentary came to be more and more concerned with exclusively eucharistic ritual and formulae.[45] It is necessary, then, to try to ascertain what sort of pontifical Aquinas might have known.

We know, for example, that the *Romano-Germanic Pontifical* (RGP) of the tenth century is an important starting point for tracing the subsequent liturgical evolution of western churches.[46] We also know that this pontifical, in a variety of redactions, enjoyed an extraordinary popularity and was widely diffused throughout continental Europe and England.[47] Moreover, we know that by the late eleventh century (during the reign of Gregory VII, 1073–1085), there is unquestionable evidence that the RGP had made its influence felt on the liturgy in Rome. Finally, by the twelfth century it had become definitively romanized.[48] It was, therefore, in Rome itself that the RGP became the immediate archetype of later pontificals of the Latin rite.[49]

In the light of developments like these one has to understand

the formation of the Roman pontificals of the twelfth and thirteenth centuries, the books which, in my opinion, Aquinas might
have known and commented upon. But some problems arise. It is
unlikely that anything like a single official Roman pontifical
existed in the twelfth century. On the contrary, all the evidence
points to the existence of numerous versions of pontifical books
for the various urban and suburban Roman churches.[50] Indeed,
these form a kind of family of texts, some nearer and some more
remote from the RGP. Despite these divergences, however, Cyril
Vogel maintains that the common source for all the Roman
episcopal books of the twelfth century was the RGP.[51] Michel
Andrieu, in his edition of the twelfth century *Roman Pontifical,*
has illustrated this dependency by printing in small letters all those
elements which were borrowed from RGP, which can thus be
considered a kind of archetype.[52]

The diffusion of the *Roman Pontifical* of the twelfth century
among churches of the West was aided by political circumstances.[53] After the reform-oriented Lateran Council of 1123
A.D., the papacy had begun to assume a more direct control over
liturgical rites as well as over the appointment of worthy
bishops.[54] Further, during the course of the twelfth century many
popes were forced to seek refuge outside Rome, usually in other
Italian cities or in France.[55] Andrieu notes that Urban II, Paschal
II, Calixtus II and Innocent II all spent time in France, conse-
crating churches, ordaining bishops, and convoking synods.[56] It is,
therefore, probable that the *Roman Pontifical* of the twelfth
century spread rather rapidly, particularly in France. Indeed, of all
the witnesses to this document, only one can be clearly traced to
Rome itself.[57]

An examination of the nine principal manuscripts used by
Andrieu reveals an interesting geographical dispersion of this
Roman Pontifical:

1. *Grenoble Cod.140:* probably originated at Grenoble some-
time after 1170 and contains a rite for baptism on Holy Saturday.[58]
2. *London Brit. Mus. Cod. Add. 17005:* from the province of
Mainz, in the early thirteenth century, has an *ordo ad consignandos pueros.*[59]

3. *Lyons Bibl. municip. Cod. 570:* a composite text originating about 1214, probably from the northern part of France, has a rite *ad confirmandos infantes.*[60]

4. *Rome Vat. Cod. Lat. 7114:* a composite text, probably from the province of Acquitaine, in the second half of the thirteenth century, has at least part of a confirmation rite (with the form *Confirmo et consigno te signo sancte crucis in nomine patris et filii et spiritus sancti*).[61]

5. *Rome Vat. Cod. Lat. 8718:* for the most part from the twelfth century, probably from the church of Chieti in the Abruzzi, has two sets of orations for confirmation.[62]

6. *Rome Vat. Cod. Barb. 631:* probably from Monte Cassino, near the end of the eleventh century, has orders for baptism and confirmation on Holy Saturday.[63]

7. *Rome Vat. Cod. Borghes. Lat. 49:* probably from Sora, early in the thirteenth century, has an order for baptism on Holy Saturday, plus an *ordo ad consignandos infantes ab episcopo* which closely resembles the order prescribed in the Pontifical of the Roman Curia of the thirteenth century.[64]

8. *Rome Vat. Ottobon. Lat. 270:* from Rome, has an *ordo ad consignandos pueros.*[65]

9. *Troyes Bibl. municip. Cod. 2272:* from the region of Clairvaux (or some other Benedictine abbey in the area of Lombardy), and probably from the late eleventh century, has a rite entitled *Confirmatio puerorum.*[66]

This distribution of manuscripts reveals two important points: the *Roman Pontifical* of the twelfth century was widespread in Europe and it contained a rite for confirmation, or "consignation," a rite variously allied to and independent of the baptismal office of Holy Saturday.

In Andrieu's edition, the paschal rites of initiation follow this sequence.[67] (1) After terce of Holy Saturday, those to be baptized go to church. There follows a *redditio* of the Creed and the Lord's prayer, a signing with the cross by the *sacerdos* on the foreheads of the candidates with the words, *in nomine patris et filii et spiritus sancti.* (2) Next comes a prayer of exorcism, *imposita manu super capita singulorum,* and (3) the *Effeta,* in which the nostrils and ears are touched with spittle. These in turn are followed by (4) a renunciation of Satan, and (5) an anointing with holy oil on the breast and between the shoulders of the candidates. (6) Then the Creed and Lord's prayer are said over the candidates *imposita manu*. (7) After these come the blessing of the baptismal font, (8) the baptism with credal interrogations and a triple immersion. (9) The *patrinus* next presents the candidate to the priest or bishop, who proceeds to sign the infant with chrism. (10) The neophyte is clothed with a white garment and (11) presented with a candle. (12) If the bishop is present, he immediately confirms with chrism and communicates the infant (*statim oportet eum confirmare chrismate et communicari secundum consuetudinem quarumdam ecclesiarum*). (13) There follows the text of an *ordo ad consignandos infantes*.

In all the above thirteen points, except 6, 9, 11, 12 and 13, the rite seems to follow, wholly or in part, that of RGP.

My own opinion is that the rite of confirmation known to Aquinas would have been based on some version of the twelfth-century *Roman Pontifical*. While it is true that the twelfth-century book yielded place to the *Roman Curial Pontifical* of the thirteenth-century, there is one factor especially which leads me to suggest that the twelfth and not the thirteenth-century books would have been known to Thomas. The factor concerns the dating of the latter pontifical. According to Andrieu's analysis, the first recension of the thirteenth-century book stems from the beginning of that century, while the second recension appeared about fifty years later. It was the second recension which was eventually to predominate.[68] Of the two descriptions of confirmation in the thirteenth-century pontifical, the second stems primarily from manuscripts of the fourteenth century.[69] Finally, most of the manuscripts of the thirteenth-century pontifical described by Andrieu date from the *late* decades of that century or from the fourteenth century,[70] which would postdate Aquinas, who died in 1274.[71]

It seems plausible to me, therefore, that the rite of confirmation known to Aquinas would have been the one contained in some version of the *Roman Pontifical of the Twelfth Century*. The following points support this hypothesis: the geographical diffusion of the twelfth-century book outside the city of Rome makes it quite feasible that it could have been used in churches with which Thomas was familiar; 2) the dating factor for the thirteenth century pontifical and for the pontifical of Durandus seems to eliminate them from possible knowledge by Aquinas; 3) the rites which Thomas describes, somewhat fragmentarily, for baptism (IIIa, 71; IIIa, 66, 10) and for confirmation (IIIa, 72) are not inconsistent with those outlined above for the twelfth-century pontifical; 4) even though there is some evidence for a kind of "incipient Gallicanism" among the French clergy of the thirteenth century,[72] it does not mean that the Roman books were not used there. Besides, Aquinas was a staunch defender of the papacy and of the notion of *plenitudo potestatis*. As a mendicant friar, furthermore, he would naturally have been in sympathy with the popes of this period, most of whom defended the rights and privileges of the friars, especially during the controversies at the University of Paris.

We turn now to the sacramental theology which Aquinas mounted on the ritual he knew. His views on the structure and meaning of sacraments are rich, subtle, and varied. A thumb-nail summary of those views would reveal the following characteristics:

Thomas argues that sacraments have no meaning apart from the life of man: "the life of the spirit is conformed to the life of the body."[73] Christian sacramental life thus takes its concrete shape and pattern from the analogy with human bodily life. This principle, which will play a very prominent role in Thomas' theology of confirmation, is related both to the structures of human growth and perception and to the theology of the incarnation. A passage from the *Compendium Theologiae* exemplifies this point:

> It is common to all the sacraments that they consist of bodily words and deeds just as in Christ, the source of sacraments, the Word has become flesh. Just as the flesh of Christ has the power to sanctify and was itself sanctified through union with the Word, so too sacraments are sanctified and derive their power of sanctification through the words which are proclaimed in them.[74]

The taproot for Aquinas' view of the sacraments is a strong Christian anthropology, coupled with a sturdy emphasis on the power of the Word proclaimed in those sacraments.

Thomas is vigorously aware, too, of the social dimension of sacraments. His theology of baptism stresses the believer's communion with Christ as head of the ecclesial body[75] and with the gathered assembly.[76] Moreover, Aquinas sees baptism as a relational act which establishes the Christian's identity by rendering him a "liturgical person."[77] By the same token, social relation and personal communion are the keynotes of Thomas' view of *character* in the sacraments. Indeed, one might translate his conception of baptismal character in this way: it is the unfolding of a dynamism in human life ordered to the expression, through worship, of precisely who and what man is in relation to the mystery of God. The character of Christian baptism is not an objectified thing but a relationship which establishes a permanent connection between Christ, the believer, and cult. That is why Thomas is concerned to point out that baptismal character is to be understood primarily in terms of personal communion with Christ and Christ's body corporate. He sums up the matter with lapidary precision: "the everlasting character (of the sacraments) is Christ himself."[78] Use of the vocabulary of 'character' is simply Aquinas' way of articulating the biblical image of God's People as permanently "royal, priestly and holy."[79]

Finally, Aquinas is well acquainted with the Greek patristic notion that sacraments effect the deification (*theopoiesis*) of men,[80] but he resists the temptation to understand the deification solely on the model of incarnation. His analysis of sacramental action has a perceptible pneumatological cast. This is the reason why Thomas sees the "new law of the gospel" as nothing less than "the grace of the Holy Spirit given to the heart of the believer."[81] For him the sacraments effect grace neither out of their own power nor out of human agency, but because of the saving work done for men by God in Christ and communicated through the Spirit.

This pneumatological bent of Aquinas' sacramental theology is critical for understanding what he means by that old bugaboo *ex opere operato*. Fundamentally, *ex opere operato* is a way of expressing the permanent availability and universality of God's salvation in Christ. It is also a way of describing the inseparable relation between charism and institution. Since the new law of the gospel *is* the grace of the Holy Spirit, Christian sacramental worship insures that *both* gospel *and* grace will remain in the public sector where they can be seen, touched, tasted, handled, smelled, and celebrated. In a sense, *ex opere operato* is insurance against the illusions of a style of Christianity that always threatens to go private, sectarian, and gnostic.

✓ The split between baptism and confirmation raised not only a ritual problem but a theological one as well. We have already noticed how the relation between the effects of baptism and those of episcopal consignation concerned Rabanus Maurus in the ninth century and it concerned the scholastics of the twelfth and thirteenth centuries too. When the medieval theologians tried to make sense of confirmation three questions in particular bothered them: the search for a scriptural warrant, a "charter event," which would provide solid biblical foundation for the rite of episcopal confirmation; the need for ecclesiastical precedent and authority to support the practice; and the debate over why confirmation had effects for Christian life different from those of baptism. Here we shall be concerned to see how Aquinas resolved those problems.

Prior to Thomas, most medieval theologians tried to seek a scriptural justification for confirmation in Old Testament examples of anointing, especially in the three references to David's anointing found in the I and II Books of Samuel.[82] The effort was largely unconvincing, and Thomas must have recognized this, for he slyly dismisses all Old Testament types for confirmation by arguing that since confirmation is the "sacrament of the fulness of grace," it could have no reflection in the old, imperfect Law.[83]

Thomas probably held a minority opinion about the Old Testament types for confirmation, but apparently that did not bother him. His view about the New Testament evidence seems, likewise, to have been in the minority. The more widespread view in Aquinas' day was that confirmation was not instituted directly by Christ, but indirectly by the apostles. Such worthies as Roland Blandinelli, later Pope Alexander III, and Bonaventure supported this position, as did lesser luminaries like William of Auxerre. [84] But Aquinas dissented, commenting somewhat drily that while the apostles were indeed "pillars of the church," they were not "legislators."[85] Thomas preferred to say that Christ instituted confirmation not by means of a direct act, but by means of a promise. [86]

Although having the advantage of anchoring the sacrament in an explicit promise of Christ, this interpretation created problems of its own. I made reference above to the tendency to displace the emphasis on imposition of hands by stressing the act of anointing with chrism. The displacement was thoroughly accomplished by Aquinas' time, and he clearly regards chrism as the *materia* of the sacrament.[87] But this left him in a quandary. He obviously found it difficult to answer the objection that there is no solid New Testament evidence for the use of chrism by Christ or by the apostles in conferring the Spirit. So he attempts the typical scholastic punt by appealing to the distinction between *res* and *sacramentum*, between the inner content of grace and the sacramental sign itself. He concludes that Christ communicated the *res* of confirmation to the apostles without the use of a sacramental sign.[88]

Aquinas also had his woes when he turned to the matter of ecclesiastical precedent for the support of a separate rite of episcopal confirmation. But here the medieval lack of historical perspective eased the situation. Several times in the course of his comments Thomas refers to authorities like "Melchiades papa" or "Eusebius papa."[89] What Thomas has used are, of course, a part of the infamous false decretals, a collection of spurious papal and conciliar material which was widely circulated under the name of Isidore of Seville, but which in fact dates from ca. 850 A.D.[90] Like many another medieval theologian, Aquinas accepted this collection as genuine, partly because it had been incorporated by Gratian in his *Decretum* written about 1140 A.D.[91]

The fact that Thomas relies so heavily on "Melchiades" as an ecclesiastical precedent for confirmation certainly damages his argumentation in the eyes of contemporary readers. It would not be so damaging if he had merely cited these decretals as illustrative of a position which he had already developed and defended on other grounds. But it is clear that Aquinas depended upon Melchiades' so-called "Letter to the Spanish Bishops" as a major source for some of his most seminal ideas concerning the origin, nature, and interpretation of the sacrament.[92] Indeed, it was from the spurious text of Melchiades that Thomas obtained two central ideas in his confirmation repertoire: the notion of "increase" or "fulness" (*augmentum, plenitudo*) and the notion of "grace for strengthening" (*gratia ad robur*). The military analogy is also strong in the Melchiades text, although it had been used long before by John Chrysostom and others[93] in reference to initiation.

Use of the false decretals dogs Thomas' theology elsewhere as well, for he cites "Urbanus papa" in support of the notion that only through confirmation do persons become "full-fledged Christians."[94] It was a common medieval objection that baptized, but unconfirmed, persons were not "full Christians." Since, however, even the most hardened theologians shrank from the idea that baptized people were somehow not fully Christian, they began to distinguish various types of "fulness." Aquinas assumes this language of plenitude, arguing that confirmation consists in an augmentation of that embryonic impulse toward growth in Christian life bestowed in baptism.[95] But nowhere does Thomas deny that the Spirit is communicated to the believer in the baptismal washing. Indeed he maintains quite explicitly that the Spirit is given in the waters of baptism.[96]

Further, Thomas' use of a vocabulary of "fulness" or "augmentation" provides us with a transition to the medieval question about the related effects of baptism and confirmation. The territory here is familiar. Using the anthropological model, according to which the acts of a child mature into acts appropriate to adulthood, Aquinas argues that the power given by baptismal character corresponds to spiritual childhood, while the character of confirmation pertains to spiritual maturity.[97] Hence, Thomas sets up a kind of proportion:

baptism:confirmation ∷ human generation:human growth and maturity.[98]

Central to Thomas' notion of confirmation is, then, the idea of a "perfect age," of "spiritual adulthood." But this is open to misunderstanding. For Aquinas, "spiritual adulthood" is not chronological; the grace of the sacrament of confirmation makes even an infant "spiritually mature." Thomas' notion of maturity relates not to the human conditions of age or perception, but to the limitless transforming power of grace.[99]

M. Magrassi has pointed out that Aquinas' concept of spiritual adulthood actually implies two levels of development: the structural, existential level according to which a human being is gradually led to integrate his personality and to emerge as a stable adult; and the dynamic and social level, according to which a person begins to assume all the social responsibilities of adult maturity.[100]

These two levels of development in the human organism are reflected, Magrassi suggests, in Aquinas' view of the supernatural organism which is constituted by the life of grace. The rather fragile life of the baptized Christian develops into a more perfect configuration to Christ under the fructifying action of the Holy Spirit.[101] The theological model for this development is, of course, Christ himself, from whom all the sacraments derive their power to sanctify.[102] Although Jesus was "full of grace and truth" from the first instant of his conception, that fulness, Thomas maintains, was not publicly manifested until the baptism by John in the Jordan.[103]

Thus Aquinas distinguishes confirmation from baptism by using the notion of spiritual adulthood to define, analogically, what happens in the sacramental character of confirmation: the Christian, justified in baptism, is given the "fulness of grace" in confirmation. This "fulness" is, in Thomas' opinion, the *res* or inner content of the sacrament of confirmation,[104] just as the *res* of baptism is justification.[105] The theological distinction between the two sacraments is based on a difference in their respective sacramental *res:* baptism gives justifying grace, whereas confirmation gives "fulness of grace." The analogy between the human organism and the supernatural organism of grace is at the root of this distinction:

human organism:	supernatural organism:
conception, birth— ::	justifying grace (baptism)—
full maturity	fulness of grace (confirmation)

For Thomas, confirmation "perfects" baptism, that is, it brings the life of grace to full maturity, much as human maturity perfects the inchoate biological organism. One can detect a kinship between Aquinas' position and current debates, perhaps sterile ones, over the appropriate age for confirmation.

We have arrived at the end of our consideration of the historical period from the seventh to the late thirteenth centuries. Now we shall consider some of the reasons why the Western Church found it impossible to maintain the integrity of the rite of Christian initiation. Once again, an exhaustive list is not possible. A thorough investigation would need to identify not only the liturgical sources which betray evidence of disintegrating practices of initiation in the West, but also those underlying social, political, and even economic factors which assisted the decline.

For example, Peter Brown has pointed out how the late Roman town tended to collapse inward around the local bishop, a phenomenon that can be seen happening in North Africa already in Augustine's lifetime. [106] The bishop—or in places like fifth-century Syria, the "holy man"—represented a point of stabilization in a period of acute political dislocation. [107] If one takes seriously Aquinas' point about the relational aspect of sacraments like baptism, then clearly a fluid pattern of relations in the church will tend to modify the significance of initiation. Sacraments always need to be seen in relation to particular ecclesiological models. Avery Dulles' recent *Models of the Church* might provide a starting point for examining the connection between conceptual models of church life and sacramental praxis.[108]

Besides the question of church models and structures, other factors have to be taken into account: factors which shed light on the way rituals evolve, function, malfunction, and fail. With respect to the dismemberment of Christian initiation, the following points need to be considered:

The problem of "accumulated symbolism."

Today research in the areas of anthropology and history of religions has led us to value the rich ambiguity of symbols, with their ambivalent, multi-dimensional character. Such emphasis is important and useful. But there also exists what I would like to call a "law of accumulated symbolism." There is a limit to the amount of symbolic ambiguity a rite can sustain. When the symbolic ambiguity grows too intense, when it begins to look like a tropical rain forest, then the basic architecture of the rite will begin to crumble. Paul Ricoeur has noted something of the same thing in speaking of the "polysemy" of language. The use of language demands a field of expansion, which allows for things like metaphoric and mythopoetic speech, as well as a field of limitation which prevents speech from becoming so elastic that it is useless.[109]

My argument is that in the case of such things as initiation and, especially, ordination, this "law of accumulated symbolism" came into play with a vengeance. For example, consider the case of presbyteral ordination in the West. The primitive architecture of the rite is fairly simple and discernible from Hippolytus to the *Sacramentarium Veronense*. [110] It involved laying on of hands and prayer, and not much else. Thus, the *Veronense* gives us a basic "Roman core" of three prayers: an "invitatory" (invitation to prayer before the litany), a "concluding prayer after the litany," and a prayer of ordination. [111] As the concept of the presbyteral office developed, however, the rite absorbed symbolic accretions from every direction (anointings, complicated ceremonials of investiture, etc.). Thus it is not surprising that by the time of the RGP (ca. 950 A.D.), the ancient, intimate relation between laying on of hands and prayer had been obscured. [112] In order to handle the massive accumulation of symbolism, the rite had been fractured into a series of acts denoting the communication of powers. The earlier, more straightforward rite was unable to ingest such accumulations of symbolism and its unity was inexorably lost.

Somewhat the same thing happened with Christian initiation. The various symbolisms of washing, sealing, incorporation, death-resurrection are clustered around a central axis: the paschal mystery of Jesus. In itself, this would present no problem. As long as people understand, through catechesis, how the various symbolisms in the cluster are related, the rite can maintain its cohesiveness. But such a cluster of accumulated symbols will begin to split apart if adequate catechesis declines.

We see this happening as we progress into the medieval period where Christian initiation becomes rife with symbols for the communication of the Holy Spirit to the believer (laying on of hands, anointings, acts of sealing, etc.). But it is also clear that even the most perceptive medieval theologians no longer understand how the symbolic cluster associated with "bestowing the Spirit" relates to the symbolic cluster associated with "incorporation into Christ." A man like Rabanus Maurus, as we saw, began casting about for some way to distinguish the effect of the first anointing after baptism (presbyteral) from the effect of the second anointing (episcopal). [113] As discussed earlier, he arrived at the formulation that the first anointing brings the descent of the Spirit while the second brings the grace of the Spirit "with fulness of sanctity, knowledge and power." The stage is thereby set both theologically and ritually for constructing a rationale for the split between a "baptismal cluster" of rites and a "pneumatic cluster" of rites associated with confirmation. The "law of accumulated symbolism" has done its work: the heavy symbolism of Christian initiation has, under the influence of declining catechesis and theological misunderstanding, forced the original architecture of the rite to collapse into two "separate and distinct sacraments" with "separate and distinct effects."

Loss of symbolic intelligibility.

In a recent series of articles, J. Brinkman has spent some time analyzing what he calls the "heuristic" dimension of symbols. [114] By "heuristic," Brinkman means the "triggering" effect which symbols exhibit, their ability to set off a kind of chain reaction in the perceiver, a reaction that leads him into further and further symbolic associations. For example, if we think of the bread-symbolism of the eucharist, a chain of symbolic associations is set up: bread, food, nourishment, body, body of Christ, body of the church, etc. A good symbol always manifests this heuristic aspect, this capacity for drawing one deeper and deeper into the symbolic implications of a word, a gesture, a material object. The heuristic dimension of a symbol is directly related to its intelligibility. Unless the symbol can trigger this chain of associations, it will remain a sort of Zwinglian *nudum signum*.

Christian initiation is full of heuristic symbolism, but that symbolism is intelligible only if the perceiver can link up the symbol with the elements of his own experience. Water symbolism in initiation for instance should operate in this heuristic manner. If, on the other hand, one's chief experience of water is "pollution" or "chlorine," then the triggering effect of the symbolism is lost. Or if one's contact with water in the symbolic gesture is minimal (e.g., a few drops poured out of a plaster sea-shell), a similar loss of the heuristic power of the symbol is inevitable.

Loss of the tactile dimension.

Sacraments are a form of intimate behavior in the sense that they involve tactile liberties that might provoke arrest anywhere else. There is, I suspect, a direct correlation between the loss of the tactile dimension of sacramental gestures and their progressive cerebralization. In the earlier celebration of Christian initiation, the tactile dimension was strong, for there was total immersion in water, rubbing with oil, nudity, imposition of hands, kissing. This does not mean that early Christian baptism was a massive sensitivity phenomenon, but it does mean that the symbolic power of initiation (including the "heuristic" power noted above) was closely allied with a series of tactile contacts. When those contacts are severely minimalized, there is a tendency to replace tactile conversation with verbal conversation. Rather than doing, we begin to talk about doing. Perhaps this helps to explain why, in the medieval period, there was a general tendency to replace the tactile dimension of sacramental acts with a visual dimension, for the liturgy was seen as the *dramatic* enactment of a past event.[115]

Misunderstanding of the connection between memorial (anamnesis) and invocation (epiclesis) in worship.

Every sacramental act involves both memorial and invocation, and it is of critical importance to understand how these two are connected. If "memorial" is understood merely as the dramatic recital of past events, then "invocation" will be interpreted as a calling upon the Spirit to vivify what would otherwise remain dead narration. But to understand the relation between *anamnesis* and *epiclesis* in this fashion is artificial and misleading. Scholars have long recognized this problem, and various theories have been advanced with an eye to rehabilitating the notion of memorial. One thinks, for example, of Odo Casel's *Mysterientheologie*. [116]

Such "re-presentation" theories attempt to see in the sacramental memorial the acts of Christ "re-presented" and thereby rendered available to the present experience of believers. So understood, sacraments are not dramatic re-enactments, but rather the renewed presentation of the power and efficacy of charter events like the Last Supper, Cross, Resurrection, etc.

But representation theories do not quite get to the heart of the matter, nor do they really clarify the relation between memorial and invocation in worship. A look at Augustine's experience may offer some light on the subject. [117] Augustine discovered that the God he sought lived at the *interior* of his human memory. The *Confessions* do not represent an effort to dredge up dead memories of the living God; rather, they recognize that God is intimately present within the very structure of human memory. Augustine discovered that memory is a form of transcendence, that the journey through memory is a journey in God's immediate presence. To remember, to "do God's memorial," is already invocation (*epiclesis*). Memorial and invocation, *anamnesis* and *epiclesis,* are one, since the memory of God is possible only through the action of the Spirit in the depths of the human heart. Perhaps this is the reason why the *Confessions* constantly moves back and forth between personal recollections and invocations of prayer.

What Augustine discovered on the level of personal experience can, *mutatis mutandis,* be said about the relation between the community's memory and its invocation of the Spirit. The Spirit is not invoked to vivify the dead recital of past deeds, but rather to exhibit God's presence as intimately interior to the community's act of memory. The purpose of epicletic invocation in the sacraments is *not* to supply something lacking in memorial, but to reveal in the external life of the Christian people what is already enfleshed in their collective memory. *Anamnesis* and *epiclesis* in the sacraments are not separable items; they are the "outside" and the "inside" of a single reality—the reality of God's Word *become* flesh, the reality of Christ's broken body *becoming* a body corporate. Thus to "do the memorial of Christ's Pasch" in the Christian eucharist is, at the same time, to invoke the Spirit who exhibits *both* gifts *and* people as the tangible flesh of what that Pasch means.

My suspicion is that a dislocation between *anamnesis* and

epiclesis aided the disintegration of Christian initiation in the West. The vocabulary of memory and invocation tended to be displaced by a language of imitation and obedience. Take for example Aquinas' view of Christ's baptism as the charter event for Christian baptism.[118] The East had made a similar appeal but with an emphasis on the idea that Christ's flesh sanctified water and made it the agent of divinization. Aquinas, on the other hand, is more concerned with deriving the instrumental efficacy of baptism from the baptism of Christ (i.e., Christ's baptism is to ours as cause is to effect). The implication here is that Christians baptize in imitation of, and in obedience to, a dominical charter event. Lost sight of is the fact that in the community's memory the baptism of Christ was, at the same time, a disclosure of his messianic identity through the power of the Spirit.

It could be argued that once baptism came to be viewed primarily as imitative behavior (as memorial in the weakest sense), it seemed more and more necessary to complete or perfect or simply finish the act of baptism by a separate, ritual act of *epiclesis*—confirmation. What confirmation became was, substantially, a "dangling *epiclesis*" cut off from the symbolic syntax which inserted believers into the dying and rising of Jesus through the paschal memorial. It was a clumsy way of attending to what western theology felt was the unfinished business of baptism.

Today we find ourselves caught with our hands full of this sort of unfinished business. Ours is a humpty-dumpty problem: all the king's horses and all the king's men have not yet succeeded in putting back together the fractured rite of Christian initiation.

NOTES

1. Latin text in A. Wilmart (ed.), *Analecta Reginensia* Studi e Testi, 59 (Città del Vaticano: Biblioteca apostolica Vaticana, 1933): 170–179. English translation (partial) in E. C. Whitaker, (ed.), *Documents of the Baptismal Liturgy*, 2nd ed., rev. and suppl. (London: S.P.C.K., 1970): 154–158.

2. For texts and translations, cf. the following: K. Lake, (ed., trans.), *The Apostolic Fathers*, Loeb Classical Library (New York: Macmillan, 1912–1913): 308–333 (with English translation). Cf. also Whitaker, *Documents*, p. I. G. Raschen, *S. Iustini apologiae duae*, Florilegium Patristicum 2,2nd ed.

(Bonn: Peter Hanstein, 1911). Partial English translation of section dealing with baptism in Whitaker, *Documents,* p. 2. B. Botte, (ed., trans.), *La Tradition Apostolique de Saint Hippolyte: Essai de Reconstitution,* Liturgie-wissenschaftliche Quellen und Forschungen 39 (Münster: Aschendorf, 1963). English translation of sections dealing with baptism in Whitaker, *Documents,* pp. 3–7.

3. J. D. C. Fisher, *Christian Initiation: Baptism in the Medieval West,* Alcuin Club Collections 47 (London: S.P.C.K., 1965), and L. L. Mitchell *Baptismal Anointing,* Alcuin Club Collections 48 (London: S.P.C.K., 1966). Both these works supply comprehensive documentation. A useful and less technical survey of the emergence of episcopal confirmation as a rite separated from baptism in the West may be found in A. P. Milner, *The Theology of Confirmation,* Theology Today Series 26 (Notre Dame, Indiana: Fides Publishers, Inc., 1971).

4. On the separation of eucharistic communion from the other acts of initiation, cf. Fisher, *Christian Initiation,* pp. 101–108.

5. Cf. M. Andrieu, (ed.), *Les Ordines Romani du haut moyen-age,* Spicilegium Sacrum Lovaniense II (Louvain: Spicilegium Sacrum Lovaniense, 1948): 380–413.

6. For the text of the *De Mysteriis,* cf. O. Faller, (ed.), *Sancti Ambrosii Opera VII,* Corpus Scriptorum Ecclesiasticorum Latinorum 73 (Vienna: Hoelder-Pichler-Tempsky, 1955): 89–116; on the *spiritale signaculum,* cf. *De Mysteriis,* 7, 42 (ed. cit., p. 106): "Unde repete quia accepisti signaculum spiritale, spiritum sapientiae et intellectus, spiritum consilii atque virtutis, spiritum cognitionis atque pietatis, spiritum sancti timoris, et serva, quod accepisti. Signavit te deus pater, confirmavit te Christus dominus, et dedit pignus, spiritum, in cordibus tuis, sicut apostolica lectione didicisti." English translation of the passage in Whitaker, *Documents,* pp. 132–133.

7. On this point, cf. L. Mitchell, *Baptismal Anointing,* pp. 88–91.

8. Cf. L. Mitchell, "Ambrosian Baptismal Rites," *Studia Liturgica* 1 (1972): 251.

9. The text of Maxentius' letter may be found in "Epistolae II" *Monumenta Germaniae Historica,* ed. E. Duemmler, (Berlin: Widemann, 1895): 537–539 (the text is also in Migne, *PL* 106. 51–54). Duemmler dates the letter, ca. 811–812. The letter does mention an imposition of hands, but that in connection with the *scrutinium* prior to baptism. Only one anointing after baptism is mentioned: ". . . deinde translati ad gremium matris ecclesiae per lavacrum regenerationis adoptionis filii effecti, scripti in libro vitae Christi domini nostri, a cuius sancto nomine chrisma nomen accepit, peruncti etiam hii huius sacrae unctionis chrisma salutis, id est sancti Spiritus largissima in Christo Iesu domino nostro in vitam aeternam" (p. 538).

10. Cf. Fisher, *Christian Initiation,* pp. 38–39.

11. *Ibid.,* p. 39.

12. *Ibid.*

13. Cf. M. Andrieu, *Le Pontifical Romain au Moyen-Age,* I: *Le Pontifical Romain du XIIe Siècle,* Studi e Testi 86 (Città del Vaticano: Biblioteca apostolica Vaticana, 1938): 246–247.

14. Thus John remarks to Senarius: "I must say plainly and at once, in case I seem to have overlooked the point, that all these things are done even to infants, who by reason of their youth understand nothing . . . " (Whitaker, *Documents,* p. 157).

15. See below, pp. 20–21 for an outline of paschal initiation in the *Roman Pontifical of the XII Century*.

16. Cf. Fisher, *Christian Initiation*, pp. 23–24.

17. The evidence for Gennadius comes from his *De Ecclesiasticis Dogmatibus* (text in Migne, *PL* 58. 979–1000). In the passage on baptism (cap. 52, cols. 993–994), Gennadius speaks about the admission of heretics who have been baptized already in the name of the Trinity. These should be admitted through the laying on of hands: ". . . purgati jam fidei integritate confirmentur manus impositione." Children ("parvuli"), Gennadius remarks, should be "strengthened by laying on of hands and chrism, and should be admitted to the mysteries of the eucharist" (". . . sic manus impositione et chrismate communiti, eucharistiae mysteriis admittantur").

18. See the discussion on the Gallican rites in L. L. Mitchell, *Baptismal Anointing*, pp. 112–125. Mitchell writes: "In sum, none of the Gallican sacramentaries includes a rite of episcopal confirmation, nor have we any evidence requiring us to assume that such a rite was customarily added to the extant baptismal rites, nor that the administration of the single Gallican post-baptismal anointing was confined to bishops" (p. 125).

19. Cf. Fisher, *Christian Initiation*, pp. 58–61.

20. Such, apparently, is the order described by Alcuin in a letter (no. 134) addressed "Oduino presbytero" and dating from about 798 A.D.: ". . . Sic corpore et sanguine dominico confirmatur, ut illius sit capitis membrum, qui pro eo passus est et resurrexit. Novissime per inpositionem manus a summo sacerdote septiformis gratiae spiritum accipit, ut roboretur per Spiritum sanctum ad praedicandum aliis, qui fuit in baptismo per gratiam vitae donatus aeternae." Text in E. Duemmler, ed., *Monumenta Germaniae Historica Epistolae*, IV, p. 203. Substantially the same thing is repeated in a letter (no. 137) to a community of monks in Septimania (cf. ed. cit., pp. 214–215). See the discussion in Fisher, *Christian Initiation*, pp. 57–62.

21. Rabanus links the bestowal of the Spirit in confirmation with the exercise of the episcopal office, as if to imply that the "fulness of the Spirit" can be bestowed only by one who possesses the "fulness of priestly order" (i.e., the bishop). Thus, he argues that, while presbyters are indeed "priests" (*sacerdotes*), they cannot perform the postbaptismal consignation with chrism on the forehead because they do not possess the "fulness of priest-hood" (*pontificatus apicem non habent*): "Sed licet sint sacerdotes, tamen pontificatus apicem non habent, quod nec chrismate frontem signavit, nec paracletum spiritum dant, quod solis episcopis deberi lectio Actus Apostolorum demonstrat . . ." Cf. Rabanus' *De Clericorum Institutione*, Book I, cap. 6 (Migne, *PL* 107. 302).

22. Cf. Rabanus Maurus, *De Clericorum Institutione*, Book I, cap. 30 (Migne, *PL* 107. 314): "Signatur enim baptizatus cum chrismate per sacerdotem in capitis summitate, per pontificem vero in fronte, ut priori unctione significetur Spiritus sancti super ipsum descensio ad habitationem Deo consecrandam, in secunda quoque ut ejusdem Spiritus sancti septiformis gratia cum omni plenitudine sanctitatis et scientiae et virtutis, venire in hominem declaretur."

23. In Book II, cap. 39 of his *De Clericorum Institutione* (Migne, *PL* 107. 353), Rabanus speaks about the annual celebration of Easter and indicates that, after a week's interval, the neophytes baptized at the Paschal Vigil receive the Holy Spirit through imposition of hands by the bishop: ". . . sep-

tem dies Albas vocitamus, propter eos qui in sancta nocte baptizati, albis per totam hebdomadam utuntur vestibus; et tunc maxime dum alba tolluntur a baptizatis vestimenta, per manus impositionem a pontifice Spiritum sanctum accipere conveniens est, qui in baptismo omnium receperunt remissionem peccatorum, et per septem dies evangelico castitatis habitu et luminibus coelestis claritatis sanctis assistere sacrificiis solent."

24. Cf. Fisher, *Christian Initiation*, p. 66, where the author criticizes Dom Gregory Dix's understanding of the historical situation in Rabanus' time.

25. Cf. Cyprian, "Letter 74" (to Pompey), especially sections 5 and 6. Latin text may be found in *S. Thasci Caecili Cypriani Epistolae Opera Omnia*, ed. by G. Martel, Corpus Scriptorum Ecclesiasticorum Latinorum 3, part 2 (Vienna: Tempsky, 1871): 802–804. For an English translation, cf. R. B. Donna, *Saint Cyprian: Letters 1–81*, The Fathers of the Church 51 (Washington, D.C.: Catholic University of America Press, 1964): 288–290.

26. *Ibid.* In attacking the position of his heretical opponents, Cyprian remarks: "Aut si effectum baptismi maiestati nominis tribuunt, ut qui in nomine Iesu Christi ubicumque et quomodocumque baptizantur innouati et sanctificati iudicentur, cur non in eiusdem Christi nomine illic et manus baptizato inponitur ad accipiendum spiritum sanctum, cur non eadem eiusdem maiestas nominis praeualet in manus inpositione quam ualuisse contendunt in baptismi sanctificatione?" (ed. Hartel, pp. 802–803). English translation in Donna, pp. 288–289.

27. Cf. Cyprian, "Letter 74," section 7: "Porro autem non per manus inpositionem quis nascitur quando accipit spiritum sanctum, sed in baptismo, ut spiritum iam natus accipiat, sicut in primo homine Adam factum est. Ante eum Deus plasmauit, tunc insufflauit in faciem eius flatum vitae" (ed. Hartel, p. 804). English translation in Donna, p. 290.

28. Cf. Milner, *Theology of Confirmation*, pp. 19–22.

29. Cf. J. P. Smith, trans., *St. Irenaeus: Proof of the Apostolic Preaching*, Ancient Christian Writers 16 (Westminster, Maryland: The Newman Press, 1952), sections 41–42 (pp. 73–74); section 47 (p. 78); section 89 (p. 102). Cf. also Irenaeus' *Adversus Haereses*, III, 18, 1–2, as in W. W. Harvey, *Sancti Irenaei episcopi Lugdunensis libros quinque Adversus Haereses*, II (Cambridge, 1857): 92–93.

30. Cf. the discussion in Milner, *Theology of Confirmation*, pp. 21–22.

31. Cf. L. Mitchell, "Ambrosian Baptismal Rites," p. 251. English translation of Beroldus' order in Whitaker, *Documents*, pp. 147–152.

32. Cf. Sermon 227 (Migne numbering). English translation is that of P. Weller, *Selected Easter Sermons of Saint Augustine* (St. Louis: B. Herder Book Co., 1959): 104–105. Latin text in Migne, *PL* 38: 1099–1101.

33. Cf. Milner, *Theology of Confirmation*, pp. 29–30.

34. Many of these materials are conveniently collected in Whitaker, *Documents*, pp. 222–230.

35. While it is not the only work wherein Aquinas speaks about confirmation, the *Summa* has obvious importance as a work of his maturity. Other works, such as the youthful *Commentary on the Sentences* or the late opusculum *De Perfectione Vitae Spiritualis* (ca. 1269–1270) are also significant for Thomas' views. Cf. A. Adam, *Das Sakrament der Firmung nach Thomas von Aquin*, Freiburger Theologische Studien 73 (Freiburg: Verlag Herder, 1957): 3.

36. References to the *Summa Theologiae* are given in standard fashion. Thus "IIIa, 72, 12" refers to "Part Three, Question 72, article 12."

37. *Summa Theologiae* IIIa, 72, 12 and IIIa, 66, 10.

38. *Summa Theologiae* IIIa, 72, 11.

39. *Summa Theologiae* IIIa, 72, 12, ad 2um.

40. *Summa Theologiae* IIIa, 72, 12, corpus.

41. Cf. M. Andrieu, *Le Pontifical Romain du XIIe Siècle*, pp. 246–247. For convenience in citation, further references to Andrieu's edition of the *Roman Pontifical of the XII Century* will be given as follows: Andrieu, RP XII, p.____.

42. Cf. C. Vogel, *Introduction aux Sources de l'Histoire du Culte chrétien au Moyen Age*, Biblioteca degli 'Studi Medievali' 1 (Spoleto: Centro Italiano di Studi sull'alto Medioevo, 1966): 183.

43. *Ibid.;* cf. also Andrieu, RP XII, pp. 15–16.

44. Cf. Vogel, *Introduction*, pp. 185–186 (a partial list of manuscripts, mostly of the 9th and 10th centuries, is given).

45. *Ibid.*, pp. 186–187.

46. Further details about the RGP may be found in Vogel, *Introduction*, pp. 190–199.

47. There even exist manuscripts of the RGP made in Poland (cf. Vogel, p. 200).

48. Cf. Vogel, *Introduction*, p. 202.

49. *Ibid.*, p. 203.

50. *Ibid.*, p. 204.

51. *Ibid.*

52. Cf. Andrieu, RP XII, *passim.*

53. *Ibid.*, p. 16.

54. *Ibid.*, p. 17.

55. *Ibid.;* cf. also Vogel, *Introduction*, p. 206.

56. Cf. Andrieu, RP XII, pp. 17–18.

57. This is Vaticanus Ottobonianus Lat. 270. *Ibid.*, p. 16; cf. Vogel, *Introduction*, p. 206.

58. Cf. Andrieu, RP XII, pp. 21–22; 26.

59. *Ibid.*, p. 28; 32.

60. *Ibid.*, p. 35; 43.

61. *Ibid.*, pp. 43–44; 51.

62. *Ibid.*, p. 52; 61.

63. *Ibid.*, p. 61; 66; 70–71.

64. *Ibid.*, pp. 74–75; 76–77.

65. *Ibid.*, pp. 77–79; 81.

66. *Ibid.*, p. 81; 88.

67. *Ibid.*, pp. 141–148.

68. Cf. M. Andrieu, *Le Pontifical Romain au Moyen-Age, II: Le Pontifical de la Curie Romaine au XIIIe Siècle*, Studi e Testi 87 (Città del Vaticano: Biblioteca apostolica Vaticana, 1940): 313–315. Hereafter, I shall cite this work as follows: Andrieu, RP XIII, p.____.

69. *Ibid.*, pp. 573–575; 319–320.

70. *Ibid.*, pp. 3–227, where a full listing of the manuscript evidence is given.

71. This dating factor also rules out the *Pontifical of William Durandus*,

which seems to date ca. 1293–1295. Further, there are no pontificals proper to the Dominican order dating from Aquinas' time; cf. Vogel, *Introduction*, pp. 208–209. It is the opinion of N. M. Denis-Boulet that the Dominicans probably adopted the rites of Paris or of other dioceses in which they were particularly active. Cf. A. Martimort, ed., *L'Eglise en Prière*, 3rd ed., rev. and corrected (Paris: Desclée, 1965): 310.

72. Cf. D. L. Couie, "The Conflict between Seculars and Mendicants in the University of Paris in the Thirteenth Century," *Papers of the Aquinas Society of London* 23, (London, 1953): 26 ff.

73. "Vita enim spiritualis conformatur vitae corporali." Cf. *Compendium Theologiae* 613. Cf. R. A. Verardo, ed., *S. Thomae Aquinatis Opuscula Theologica* (Rome: Marietti, 1954): 147. (The section cited is usually put together with the "Compendium Theologiae ad fratrem Reginaldum socium suum carissimum," written about 1270; more properly, however, it belongs to the opusculum "De Articulis Fidei et Ecclesiae Sacramentis ad Archiepiscopum Panormitanum," apparently written ca. 1261–1268.)

74. *Compendium Theologiae* 614. Author's translation. *Ibid.*, p. 148.

75. *Summa Theologiae*, IIIa, 69, 5.

76. *Summa Theologiae*, IIIa, 70, 1.

77. *Summa Theologiae*, IIIa, 63, 1.

78. "Character aeternus est ipse Christus." *Summa Theologiae*, IIIa, 63, 3 sed contra.

79. 1 Peter 2:9.

80. *Summa Theologiae*, IIIa, 61, 1.

81. *Summa Theologiae*, Ia IIae, 106, 2.

82. For a convenient collection of texts, cf. K. Lynch, *The Sacrament of Confirmation in the Early-Middle Scholastic Period* I: *Texts*, Franciscan Institute Publications; Theology Series 5 (St. Bonaventure, New York: The Franciscan Institute, 1957). One example is Alexander of Hales' *Glossa in Quatuor Libros Sententiarum*, written ca. 1224–1225, which associates confirmation with David's anointing at Hebron (cf. II Samuel 2:4); see text in Lynch, p. 1, lines 15–23.

83. "Cum confirmatio sit sacramentum plenitudinis gratiae, non potuit habere aliquid respondens in veteri lege, quia nihil ad perfectum adduxit lex." Cf. *Summa Theologiae*, IIIa, 72, 1, ad 2um.

84. Representative texts in Lynch, p. 11. Cf. also Adam, *Das Sakrament der Firmung*, p. 19.

85. Cf. Aquinas' *Comm. Super Sent.*, Dist. VII, Q. 1, Sol. 1, ad primum (ed. Quaracchi, p. 567).

86. *Summa Theologiae*, IIIa, 72, 1, ad 1um.

87. *Summa Theologiae*, IIIa, 72, 2 et 3 et 9.

88. "Contulit Apostolis rem huius sacramenti, id est plenitudinem Spiritus Sancti sine sacramento." Cf. *Summa Theologiae*, IIIa, 72, 2 ad 1um.

89. *Summa Theologiae*, IIIa, 72, 1 et 6 et 7 et 11.

90. Cf. Fisher, *Christian Initiation*, pp. 160–164.

91. *Ibid.*, p. 160.

92. Cf. for example, *Summa Theologiae*, IIIa, 71, 1, corpus.

93. Cf. John Chrysostom's *Baptismal Catechesis* V, 26–27 in the edition of A. Wenger, (ed., trans.), *Jean Chrysostome: Huit Catéchèses baptismales,*

Sources Chrétiennes 50 (Paris. Cerf. 1957): 213–214. English translation in P. Harkins, *St. John Chrysostom: Baptismal Instructions*, Ancient Christian Writers 31 (Westminster, Maryland: The Newman Press, 1963): 91–92.

94. "Pleni Christiani." Cf. *Summa Theologiae*, IIIa, 72, 11, corpus.

95. *Summa Theologiae*, IIIa, 72, 5.

96. *Summa Theologiae*, IIIa, 69, 4, sed contra.

97. *Summa Theologiae*, IIIa, 72, 5.

98. "Sic se habet confirmatio ad baptismum sicut augmentum ad generationem." Cf. *Summa Theologiae*, IIIa, 72, 6.

99. *Summa Theologiae*, IIIa, 72, 3, ad 2um.

100. Cf. M. Magrassi, "Confirmatione Baptismus perficitur," *Rivista Liturgica* 54 (1967): 434–435.

101. *Ibid.*

102. *Summa Theologiae*, IIIa, 72, 3.

103. *Summa Theologiae*, IIIa, 72, 1, ad 4um.

104. *Summa Theologiae*, IIIa, 72, 2, ad 1um.

105. *Summa Theologiae*, IIIa, 66, 1.

106. Cf. P. Brown, "The Diffusion of Manichaeism in the Roman Empire," *The Journal of Roman Studies* 59 (1969): 92–103, esp.: 101–103.

107. Cf. P. Brown, "The Rise and Function of the Holy Man in Late Antiquity," *The Journal of Roman Studies* 61 (1971): 80–101. Brown's point is intriguing, and it would prove fruitful to analyze what a shifting Church structure reveals about the impact of Christian sacraments.

108. Cf. A. Dulles, *Models of the Church* (New York: Doubleday & Co., 1974) esp. chapter 1.

109. Cf. P. Ricoeur, "Structure - Word - Event," *Philosophy Today* 12 (1968): 114–129.

110. See the texts and discussion in H. Boone Porter, *The Ordination Prayers of the Ancient Western Churches*, Alcuin Club Collections 49 (London: S.P.C.K., 1967): 1–35.

111. Cf. the texts in C. Mohlberg, (ed.), *Sacramentarium Veronense*, Rerum Ecclesiasticarum Documenta, Series Major, Fontes I (Rome: Herder, 1956): 121–122, fnn. 252–254. For discussion and interpretation, cf. B. Kleinheyer, *Die Priesterweihe im römischen Ritus*, Trierer Theologische Studien 12 (Trier: Paulinus Verlag, 1962): 26–84.

112. For the text of the presbyteral ordination rite cf. C. Vogel, (ed.), *Le Pontifical Romano-Germanique du dixième Siècle. I: Le Texte*. Studi e Testi 226 (Città del Vaticano, 1963): 28–37. Cf. also L. Brandolini, "L'Evoluzione storica dei Riti della Ordinazioni," *Ephemerides Liturgicae* 83 (1969): 67–87.

113. Cf. above, pp. 9–10.

114. Cf. J. Brinkman, "On Sacramental Man," *Heytrop Journal* 13 (1972): 371–401; 14 (1973): 5–34; 162–180; 280–306; 396–416. On "heuristic language," cf. 13 (1972): 387–390.

115. One thinks, for instance, of an increasing desire to *see* the sacramental species, with such "ocular communion" tending to displace actual sacramental communion. On this point cf. H. B. Meyer, "Die Elevation im deutschen Mittelalter und bei Luther," *Zeitschrift für katholische Theologie* 85 (1963): 162–217.

116. For a concise presentation of Casel's theory, cf. C. Davis, "Odo Casel and the Theology of Mysteries," *Worship* 34 (1960): 428–438.

117. Cf. D. Power, "Symbolism in Worship: A Survey, I," *The Way* 13 (1973): 310–324, esp. 315–317. See also J. S. Dunne, *A Search for God in Time and Memory* (New York: Macmillan, paperback edition, 1970): 46–57.

118. Cf. *Summa Theologiae*, IIIa, 66, 2.

CHAPTER IV

Christian Initiation:
The Reformation Period

Leonel L. Mitchell

THE MOST OBVIOUS THING TO SAY ABOUT THE ADULT CATECHUMENATE AT the time of the Reformation is that it did not exist, although the Catechism of the Council of Trent states:

> On adults, however, the Church has not been accustomed to confer the Sacrament of Baptism at once, but has ordained that it be deferred for a certain time.[1]

We find, for example, that in 1536 the people of the Fisher Coast in India were baptized *en masse,* in number about ten thousand, and then left without instruction or pastoral care, either before or after baptism, for six years.[2] It was among these people that St. Francis Xavier labored to teach the rudiments of the faith into which they had been baptized:

> On Sundays I assemble all the people, men and women, young and old, and get them to repeat the prayers in their own language . . . I give out the First Commandment which they repeat, and then we say all together, Jesus Christ, Son of God, grant us grace to love thee above all things. When we have asked for this grace, we recite the Pater Noster together, and then cry with one accord, Holy Mary, Mother of Jesus Christ, obtain for us grace from thy Son to enable us to keep the First Commandment. Next we say an Ave Maria, and proceed in the same manner through each of the remaining nine commandments. And just as we say Twelve Paters and Aves in honour of the twelve articles of the Creed, so we say ten Paters and Aves in honour of the ten Commandments, asking God to give us grace to keep them well.[3]

This is unquestionably catechetical instruction, but it is being given to those already Christian and might be termed 'remedial catechesis'.

The pattern was the same in South America, where Indians were baptized with only a minimal prebaptismal instruction, and the catechism was used for the instruction of both children and adults after their baptism.[4]

In 1552 the first Council of Lima declared that Indians should be admitted only to the sacraments of baptism, matrimony, and penance until they were better instructed. Permission was given to bishops to administer confirmation to them, if they thought it desirable, and many Indians were in fact confirmed. The sainted Turibio, Archbishop of Lima and Apostle of Peru, confirmed half a million people between 1584 and 1590.[5] The same council required the license of the bishop himself to admit Indians to the reception of the Eucharist, and the custom arose of admitting the most faithful to Communion annually at Easter.[6]

I cite these examples of the practice of Catholic missions to make clear exactly how dead the idea of the ancient catechumenate before baptism really was. Even in such circumstances as those in the mission fields which would lend themselves easily to the revival of the ancient discipline there was no catechumenate. The most rudimentary grasp of what they were doing sufficed to admit adults to Holy Baptism, while many never received what was considered sufficient instruction for admission to the Eucharist.

If the catechumenate was indeed dead in the sixteenth century, catechesis was a primary interest of the Christian humanists of the Renaissance. Erasmus, in his *Paraphrase on St. Matthew's Gospel*, proposed that during Lent baptized boys be required to attend catechetical sermons which would explain to them the meaning of their baptismal profession:

> Then they would be carefully examined in private by approved men whether they sufficiently retain and remember the things which the priest has taught. If they be found to retain them sufficiently, they should be asked whether they ratify what their godparents promised in their name at baptism. If they answer that they ratify them, then let that profession be renewed in a public gathering of their equals, and that with solemn ceremonies, fitting, pure, serious, and magnificent, and such things as become that profession, than which there is none

more sacred. . . . These things indeed will have greater authority if they are performed by the bishops themselves.[7]

What Erasmus proposes is a postbaptismal catechumenate. He assumes the universality of infant baptism and the impossibility of catechizing infants; therefore, he proposes his catechumenate for baptized boys "when they arrive at puberty." The "solemn ceremonies" to be "performed by the bishops themselves" were certainly understood by the Reformers to be confirmation, and we find developing in the churches of the Reformation a pattern of infant baptism, catechesis, confirmation, and admission to communion.

Late medieval rituals had instructed godparents and parents to teach their baptized children the Lord's Prayer, Hail Mary, and Apostles' Creed as a preliminary to confirmation, which by the sixteenth century was normally not administered to children under seven.[8]

The rather quaint English of the Sarum *Manuale* of 1516 illustrated the tendency:

God faders and godmodyrs of thys chylde whe charge you that ye charge the foder and te moder to kepe it from fyer and water and other perels to the age of VII yere. and that ye lerne or se yt be lerned the *Pater Noster, Aue Maria,* and *Credo.* After the lawe of all holy churche and in all goodly haste to be confirmed of my lorde of the dyocise or of hys depute.[9]

We might note that the Council of Cologne in 1536 suggested for the first time that a child should not be confirmed before the age of seven, because "he will understand, not to say remember, too little or nothing of those things that are done."[10]

There is also a tradition from Wycliffe and Hus that postbaptismal instruction is concluded with a solemn profession of faith accompanied by "the apostolic rite of the laying on of hands":

Whoever being baptized has come to the true faith and purposes to portray it in action, in adversities and reproaches, to the intent that the new birth may be seen revealed in his spirit of life and thankfulness, such a one ought to be brought to the bishop, or priest, and be confirmed. And being questioned with regard to the truths of the faith and the sacred precepts, and also with regard to his good will, his firm purpose and works of truth, he shall testify and declare that he has all such things. Such a one should be confirmed in the hope of the truth he has attained, and in deed aided by the prayers of the church, so that there may come to him an increase of the gifts of the Holy Spirit for steadfastness and the welfare of the faith. Finally, by the laying on of hands to confirm the promises of God and the truth held in virtue of the name of the Father and of his Word and the kindly Spirit, let him be received into the fellowship of the church.[11]

Luther's concern for catechetical instruction and religious literacy is well known, but he had few kind words for confirmation, which he called *Affenspeil* (monkey business) and *Gaukelwerk* (mumbo jumbo). In a sermon in 1522 he conceded:

I would permit confirmation as long as it is understood that God knows nothing of it, has said nothing about it, and that what the bishops claim for it is untrue.[12]

In 1533 he preached:

Confirmation should not be observed as the bishops desire it. Nevertheless we do not find fault if every pastor examines the faith of the children to see whether it is good and sincere, lay hands on them, and confirm them.[13]

From these concerns of Luther arose what is called the "catechetical type" (*Catechismus* or *Beichtverhör*[14]) of confirmation among Lutherans. Its focus was the preparation of communicants, and during the Reformation period this catechetical confirmation did not usually involve any concluding rite. It centered in the preaching of catechetical sermons and the reading of the catechism from the pulpit, usually before the gospel. The sermons were for the entire congregation, and were given about four times a year. The sermons themselves were preached daily, or at least several time during the week. Catechetical instruction was also conducted in connection with confession and preparation for communion. "Because the average communicant was so poorly instructed, he was to become in effect a catechumen each time he went to Communion."[15] The content of the catechesis was the Ten Commandments, the Lord's Prayer, Holy Baptism, the Lord's Supper, and the Christian Life.

Typical of the preparation for First Communion in the form of several days of catechetical review (*Beichtwochen*) is this description from 1564:

Such an examination and exercise takes place here at Onoltz-bach on weekdays for the city children at twelve o'clock, for one hour each day, between Easter and Pentecost, and for the village children who belong to the parish, on Sundays and the festivals at one o'clock during the period of Reminiscere and Exaudi. In this way all may receive the Lord's Supper on Pentecost after each one has made his confession on the previous day.[16]

The confession is presumably of faith, not of sins, as described in the Pfalz-Neuburg Church Order of 1543,[17] which directs that those who wish to receive First Communion should be publicly examined at vespers on the eves of the feasts of Easter, Pentecost, and Christmas, and if they are prepared they should be admitted.

In some places this catechetical instruction was concluded by a public rite along traditional lines, as in the Liegnitz Church Order of 1535:

When the children have matured in age and grace, they shall again be presented by the parents and sponsors to the ministers in the presence of the congregation that they may make a public confession of their faith. This is to take the place of confirmation.[18]

There is also another strain in Lutheran practice which seems to relate more directly to the Wycliffe-Hus tradition, and to the concerns of Erasmus. The central figure in this line of development is Martin Bucer, who in 1534 urged the revival of confirmation in the ancient form in which "bishops laid their hands on the baptized and thereby gave them the Holy Spirit according to the example of the apostle in Samaria, Acts 8."[19]

In 1538 Bucer was called to Hesse to reform the Church there, and his ideas were put into effect in the Zeigenhain Order of Church Discipline of that year.[20] It directed that the children who were prepared through catechetical instruction to receive First Communion should be presented by their parents and sponsors to the pastors before the congregation. The whole collegium of ministers publicly examined the children in the chief articles of the Christian faith.

When they had answered the questions and publicly surrendered themselves to Christ the Lord and His churches, the pastor shall admonish the congregation to ask the Lord, in behalf of the children, for perseverance and an increase of the Holy Spirit, and conclude this prayer with a collect.

Finally the pastor shall lay his hands upon the children, thus confirming them in the name of the Lord, and establish them in Christian fellowship. He shall thereupon also admit them to the Table of the Lord.

Repp comments:

Here Bucer was influenced also by Erasmus in establishing a confirmation rite. But he did not limit himself, as did Erasmus, to a rite in which the youths themselves made a confession of the faith which their sponsors had made for them; under Luther's influence he associated the rite also with first Communion. This is the first formal association of the rite of confirmation with the Lord's Supper.[21]

The Cassel Church Order of 1539 is based upon this, and has influenced all subsequent Lutheran practice. Consequently Bucer has been called the father of Lutheran confirmation. The Cassel rite provided this formula to accompany the imposition of hands:

Receive the Holy Spirit, protection and guard against all evil, strength and help to all goodness from the gracious hand of God the Father, Son, and Holy Spirit.[22]

Bucer is also the author of the section on the sacraments in the *Consultation* of Hermann, Archbishop of Cologne. Usually known as *Einfaltigs Bedencken,* the manuscript was composed in German in 1543 and translated into Latin in 1545 and English in 1548. A copy of the Latin version was in the library of Thomas Cranmer, Archbishop of Canterbury, and it is generally recognized as one of the sources of the *Book of Common Prayer.*

In *Einfaltigs Bedencken* baptism is administered to infants upon Sundays and other Holy Days at the celebration of the eucharist, during which the parents and godparents are expected to receive communion. Bucer recognizes that the older tradition was for the infants themselves to receive, "but seeing this custom is worn away not without a cause," he directs the parents, godparents, and kinfolk to receive the eucharist "with singular desire of the Spirit that they may receive the Communion of Christ to themselves which they obtain in baptism for their infants."[23] Bucer uses the term "catechism" to describe an exhortation of considerable length addressed to the godparents prior to the baptism of the

infants. Among the questions put to the godparents in this catechetical rite was this:

> Will ye then be godfathers to this infant, and count him for a
> very son of God, a brother and member of Christ, and as soon
> as he cometh to the use of reason, if peradventure he shall lose
> his parents, or if they shall be negligent in this behalf, will ye
> take charge of him, that he may learn the ten commandments,
> the articles of our faith, the Lord's prayer, the sacraments, both
> at home and in the congregation, that from his childhood he
> may begin to understand the mystery of baptism and the
> benefits of Christ given to him therein, and afterwards when he
> is well instructed in the religion of Christ, that he confess his
> faith in the congregation with his own mouth, and through the
> participation of Christ that he give himself to obedience
> towards God and the congregation?[24]

This is followed by an exhortation to the parents, kinfolk, and
godparents to bring the child to school when he is old enough,
"that he may be instructed more fully in the mysteries of Christ
and in other things," and generally repeats what was previously
asked. We might note too that Archbishop Hermann, for whom
Einfaltigs Bedencken was written, was the same archbishop who
presided over the Council of Cologne in 1536—the council which
had been concerned that children be old enough when they were
confirmed to understand what was happening.

It is obvious from the catechetical rite that Bucer is concerned
about the absence of the catechumenate and is making an attempt
to provide a postbaptismal catechumenate. And in the section on
confirmation Bucer reasserts his belief that the solemn personal
profession of faith before God and the congregation is of divine
institution and found in both Old and New Testaments:

> At which confession of faith and profession of obedience in the
> congregation they were to be solemnly confirmed of the congre-
> gation in religion through prayer and some token of God's
> confirmation, which under Moses consisted in sacrifices and
> oblations and, in the time of the gospel, in laying on of hands
> and participation in the supper of the Lord. . . Seeing then that
> this confession of faith and giving of ourselves to the obedience
> of Christ and commendation of his church . . . cannot be done
> in baptism, when infants be baptized it must needs be done for
> them that were baptized in their infancy, when they be meetly

well instructed of religion, and when they somewhat understand those great benefits that be given in baptisim.

But when they solemly profess their faith and obedience before the congregation the very nature of faith requireth again that the congregation pray for them solemnly and desire for them the increase of the Holy Ghost that he will confirm and preserve them in the faith of Christ and obedience of the congregation, and that he will ever lead them into all truth. And forasmuch as such prayer . . . cannot but be effectuous, it pertaineth to the ministry of the congregation to strengthen them with the confirmation of the Holy Ghost, for whom the church hath prayer. Therefore our elders following the example of Christ and the apostles, did use the laying on of hands as a sign of this confirmation.[25]

It is this purified rite of confirmation which is to be revived in Cologne, with the imposition of hands, not anointing, as its matter. It is to be administered by appointed visitors twice yearly, since the bishops cannot visit the churches that often. The office itself consists in a rather extensive catechism of the candidates taken from the Cassel Church Order, a solemn profession of faith by the young people, and the imposition of hands with prayer for the confirmation of the Holy Spirit.

It seems clear that in the Lutheran Reformation tradition a postbaptismal catechumenate was considered essential, and in the line of tradition represented by Bucer, it was a part of confirmation and admission to communion.

In the *Institutes of the Christian Religion* John Calvin made his contribution:

How I wish that we might have kept the custom which existed among the ancient Christians before this misborn wraith of a sacrament came to birth! Not that it would be a confirmation such as they fancy, which cannot be named without doing injustice to baptism; but a catechizing, in which children or those near adolescence would give an account of their faith before the church. But the best method of catechizing would be to have a manual drafted for this exercise, containing and summarizing in simple manner most of the articles of our religion, on which the whole believers' church ought to agree without controversy. A child of ten would present himself to the church to declare his confession of faith. Would be examined in each article, and answer to each; if he were ignorant of anything or insufficiently understood it, he would be taught.

Thus, while the church looks on as a witness, he would profess the one true and sincere faith, in which the believing folk with one mind worship the one God.[26]

We may note the suggestion that a set catechism was the proper method of catechesis, a suggestion apparently adopted from the Reformers by the Council of Trent, which subsequently issued its own catechism. It was Calvin's firm belief that this was the original meaning of confirmation, and in a passage added to the *Institutes* in 1543 he described his view of the primitive rite:

In early times it was the custom for the children of Christians after they had grown up to be brought before the bishop to fulfill the duty which was required of those who as adults offered themselves for baptism. For the latter sat among the catechumens until, duly instructed in the mysteries of the faith, they were able to make confession of their faith before the bishop and people. Therefore, those who had been baptized as infants, because they had not then made confession of faith before the church, were at the end of their childhood or at the beginning of adolescence again presented by their parents, and were examined by the bishop according to the form of the catechism, which was then in definite form and in common use. But in order that this act, which ought by itself to have been weighty and holy, might have more reverence and dignity, the ceremony of the laying on of hands was also added. Thus the youth, once his faith was approved, was dismissed with a solemn blessing.[27]

It is not necessary at this time to discuss Calvin's misreading of the practice of the primitive church. It is sufficient for us to see what he thought it had been, and it was this practice which came into use in the Reformed Churches. We find that Reformed practice does not differ substantially from Lutheran.

In a larger sense the whole of life in Calvin's Geneva was a catechumenate. John Knox described it as "a school of Jesus Christ," with "edification" the purpose of Calvinist worship. Calvin was a theologian who waged a lifelong battle against what he considered theological ignorance, and so the didactic element of all worship was high. At the same time the Calvinist system at Geneva subjected the populace to a discipline so rigid and so thoroughly enforced as to make the harshest novice masters grow pale.

The Church of England in the sixteenth century provided no forms at all for adult baptism. It was not until 1662 that a form for adult baptism was added to the *Book of Common Prayer,* an inclusion necessitated by the growth of the Anabaptists under Cromwell—with the result that the Restoration found large numbers of English adults unbaptized.

The *Prayer Book* of 1549 made certain changes in the pattern of Christian initiation. Since the time of Archbishop Peckham (1279–1292) confirmation had been required prior to first Communion, except in extraordinary cases. This rule was retained. At the same time the confirmation of infants was abolished. Infant confirmation had been practiced as late as 1533, when the future Queen Elizabeth was baptized and confirmed at the age of three days, and in 1536 its legitimacy had been defended by the Lower House of the Convocation of Canterbury.[28]

In 1549 a new rubric at the beginning of confirmation provides that "To the end that confirmation may be ministered to the more edifying of such as shall receive it," no one can be confirmed until he can recite the Creed, the Lord's Prayer, and the ten commandments, "and can also answer such questions of this short catechism, as the Bishop (or such as he shall appoint) shall be his discretion appose them in."[29]

A second rubric follows Calvin and Bucer in giving as a reason for observing confirmation that those baptized as infants may openly confess their faith before the church. In typical Anglican fashion, this is followed by a rubric in the medieval tradition affirming that confirmation is most appropriately administered "when children come to that age, that partly by the frailty of their own flesh, partly by the assaults of the devil, they begin to be in danger to fall into sin."

The rite itself is much more traditional than that in Bucer. It is, in fact, the *confirmatio puerorum* of the Sarum *Manuale,* with the laying on of hands substituted for the chrismation. What is of particular interest to us is that the catechism is printed between the main title and the rite, so that the catechetical instruction is seen as closely bound, not to baptism, but to confirmation.

Every parish priest is required, at least once in six weeks, to spend half an hour before evensong on some Sunday or holy day instructing and examining the children of the parish in the catechism, and to do so openly in the church. These provisions remained substantially unchanged in the 1552 *Prayer Book,* which removed the chrismation from baptism, and the signing of the forehead with the cross from confirmation.

The Anglican tradition of the Reformation period thus calls for the catechetical instruction of the youth of the parish on Sunday afternoons until they can say the catechism. Parents and employers are required to "cause their children, servants and prentices" to be present for these sessions. When the children can recite the catechism they are presented to the bishop for confirmation at his next visitation, and then admitted to the reception of the eucharist.

Bucer in his *Censura* of the *Book of Common Prayer* objected to the meagerness of its provision for catechetical instruction. He thought that learning the words of the catechism was insufficient:

> I would wish . . . that all adolescents and all young people, male and female, should attend the catechizing until they are so proficient in the doctrine of Christ that they may be excused by their pastor. . . . Catechumens ought to be placed in various classes, and all the mysteries of Christ which it is necessary to believe should with such method, diligence, and power be explained and elucidated, commended and instilled into them, as will enable each to make the quicker and fuller progress and to observe whatever the Lord has commanded.[30]

The only observable effect of this aspect of Bucer's critique was the elimination of reference in the rubrics to the requirement that priests catechize the youth every six weeks, so that it spoke instead of doing it on Sundays and holy days, presumably on all of them.

There is, of course, one group springing from the Reformation which broke sharply with the medieval practice of Christian initiation. The Anabaptists abandoned infant baptism. As a rule they did not use a rite in the conventional sense, but attempted to imitate the New Testament model of Jesus' baptism in the Jordan. The baptismal theologies of the Anabaptists are a tangled skein which I shall not attempt to unravel.[31]

Although there is no such a thing as a catechumenate in the traditional sense among the Anabaptists, the Anabaptist movement itself began with "schools" for the purpose of listening to "readers" of the Bible and discussion. It was during such a "school" meeting on January 21, 1525—the day the Anabaptists were expelled from Zurich—that George Blaurock, a priest, was baptized. This was the first rebaptism, and was done by a layman.[32]

Anabaptist baptism has a revivalistic character which marks the separation of the "gathered church" of the faithful from the "world" of Papists and Protestants. Rebaptism and the sharing of bread and wine in a Lord's Supper imitative of New Testament accounts were their signs of fellowship. Baptism, now associated with confession of sins rather than of faith, had taken the place of penance in the lives of the converts. Thus the experience of forgiveness was followed by the ministration of baptism.

Basic to their belief was the conviction that all who had been so baptized were compelled by the great commission of Matthew 28:19–20 to proclaim true repentance and true baptism among all peoples. Of course, the Anabaptists were concerned to instruct their converts in their teachings, but do not seem to have had any organized catechumenate. For example, the spiritualist Caspar Schwenkenfeld criticized the Anabaptist Pilgram Marpeck for not insisting on an adequate catechumenate before baptism. Marpeck replied that such a period was unnecessary since repentance was brought through the Gospel as a work of God and not through any work of man.[33] It was the Anabaptist stance that the experience of conversion and the assurance of forgiveness were the essential preparation for baptism.

Somewhat unique is the case of Balthasar Hubmaier's *Eine Form zu Taufen* as used at Nicholsberg, which contains these instructions:

> Whoever desires to receive water baptism should first present himself to his bishop so that he may be tested as to whether he is sufficiently instructed in the articles of the law, Gospel, and faith, and in the Christian life. Also he must give evidence that he can pray, and that he can intelligently explain the articles of the Christian faith. This must all be ascertained about the candidate before he can be permitted to be incorporated into the church of Christ through external baptism unto the forgiveness of sins. If he meets these requirements the bishop then presents him to his church.[34]

Hubmaier expected that the candidates for baptism must be at least seven years of age,[35] and the rite he provides is in sharp contrast to the informal solemnity of most Anabaptist baptisms. The candidates were asked to respond "I believe" to the three paragraphs of the Apostles' Creed, to renounce the devil, to accept baptism, and to submit to the discipline of the church. The water-baptism was followed by the prayers of the church and the imposition of hands by the bishop, with the form:

> I give thee witness and authority, that thou henceforth shalt be numbered among the fellowship of Christians; that as a member of this fellowship thou shalt break bread and pray with the other Christian sisters and brethren, God be with thee and with thy spirit. Amen.[36]

Hubmaier also anticipated the dedication of children born to Anabaptist parents in a service in which the church would join the parents in praying God's blessings upon the child.[37] It seems likely that Hubmaier had in mind not so much the conversion of adults to the Anabaptist faith as the raising of children within that fellowship. This particular pattern of Christian initiation, although separated from the sacramental theology and ecclesiology which produced it, has been seen by many contemporary Christians as an appropriate one for the present age.

The presence of children for first generation Anabaptists of course produced a need and a demand for a system of catechetical instruction, but this was in fact a question of religious education rather than of a catechumenate. The Anabaptists were aware of the early catechumenate, using its existence in arguments against pedobaptists, but did not seem to have the institution themselves. They were, in fact, much more experience-oriented than either traditional Catholics or Protestants and less given to systematic expositions. George H. Williams' book *The Radical Reformation* cites examples of Anabaptist catechisms and educational systems,[38] and from these it can be seen that although they did not ritualize it, they took the catechumenal status of their children seriously.

The Anabaptist pattern of the dedication of infants with subsequent religious instruction and followed by adult baptism is today exercising a strong attraction for many whose religious heritage includes a commitment to infant baptism.[39] Certainly this practice provides a needed critique of our inherited forms. However, we must point out that in practice its "adult" character tended not to maintain itself beyond the first generation, as seen from Hubmaier's suggestion that the "believers" must be at least seven years old. Nonetheless, this pattern does position baptism, not confirmation, at the conclusion of the catechetical instruction of its "birthright members." For Anabaptists the baptismal practice was attached to a "gathered church" ecclesiology and a sacramentarian theology which denied that baptism was a means of grace. Those who advocate its readoption today must face the question of whether it can survive as an expression of a more orthodox theology of church and sacraments.

In conclusion, we can observe that the Reformation period was marked by a revival of catechetical instruction associated with confirmation rather than with baptism. And with the exception of radicals looking for the spiritual experience of forgiveness and an assurance of the candidates' inability to sin, catechetical instruction was seen almost exclusively in educational terms. While many of the baptismal rites of the Reformation Churches still contain the ritual portions of the old catechumenate, exorcisms, signings, etc., these tend to disappear in the second revision of the rite,[40] and are simple relics of past custom just as they were in the Roman ritual which made infants catechumens moments before their baptism.

Even in mission lands in the Americas or the Far East no serious attention was given to the question of adult baptism either by Catholics or Protestants outside of the Anabaptist tradition. And although the concept of the adult catechumenate was not revived for converts from paganism, the medieval practice of mass baptisms with little or no prior instruction was followed.

There was an interest in religious education, stemming from the Renaissance and from the profound conviction of many of the Reformers that their people were either theologically illiterate or grossly miseducated. And although it frequently used catechetical terms, it did not usually think of itself as a catechumenate.

The attempt to establish a preconfirmation catechumenate can best be seen as a serious attempt to adapt church institutions to the changed conditions of the modern world. And if it has largely broken down in the face of the new changes of the nineteenth and twentieth centuries, that should not blind us to the real value it had in the sixteenth. Baptism, catechesis, confirmation, first communion was the pattern which emerged from the Anglican, Lutheran, and Reformed traditions. There were substantial differences of understanding as to the nature of confirmation among and within the groups, but the pattern remained intact until this century. Pastoral concern produces this pattern, and if pastoral concern today causes us to question both the pattern and its theological basis, it can still serve as a model of the adaptability of the Christian Church to radically altered circumstances.

NOTES

1. *Catechism of the Council of Trent*, trans. J. A. McHugh and C. J. Callan (New York: Wagner, 1934): 179.

2. Stephen Neill, *A History of the Christian Missions*, Pelican History of the Church 6 (Baltimore: Penguin Books, 1964): 149.

3. Neill, *History*, p. 150.

4. Owen Chadwick, *The Reformation*, Pelican History of the Church 3 (Baltimore: Penguin Books, 1964): 329.

5. *Ibid.*

6. Neill, *History*, p. 173.

7. Paraphrase on St. Matthew's Gospel, quoted in J. D. C. Fisher, *Christian Initiation: The Reformation Period*, Alcuin Club Collections 51 (London: S.P.C.K., 1970): 169. Cf. also W. Lockton, "The Age for Confirmation," *Church Quarterly Review* 100 (1925): 27–64.

8. L. L. Mitchell, "What is Confirmation?" *Anglican Theological Review* 55 (1973): 202ff.

9. *Manuale ad usum Percelebris Ecclesie Sarisburiensis*, ed. A. J. Collins, Henry Bradshaw Society 91 (Chichester: Henry Bradshaw Society, 1960): 32.

10. Mansi, *Conciliorum Omnium Amplissima Collectio* 32, Col. 1258 (Leipzig: Walter) For English see Fisher, *Christian Initiation: The Reformation Period*, p. 185.

11. *Confessio Fidei Fratrum Waldensium.* English translation quoted in Fisher, *Christian Initiation: The Reformation Period*, p. 168.

12. *Uom Eelichen Leben* ("Sermon on Married Life") quoted in Arthur C. Repp, *Confirmation in the Lutheran Church* (St. Louis: Concordia Press, 1964): 17.

13. *Predigt am Sontag Latare Nachmittags*, quoted in Repp, *Confirmation*, p. 17.

14. In this entire section I am following Arthur Repp's excellent discussion in chapter one of his *Confirmation in the Lutheran Church*.

15. *Ibid.*, p. 22.
16. George Karg, quoted in Repp, *Confirmation*, p. 25.
17. Aemilius Ludwig Richter (ed.), *Die evangelischen Kirchenordnungen des sechszehnten Jahrhunderts* (Nieuwkoop: B. de Graaf, 1967): 27.
18. Repp, *Confirmation*, p. 45.
19. E. A. Achelis, *Lehrbuch der Praktischen Theologie* 2 (Leipzig: J. C. Hinrichs, 1911): 315.
20. E. Sehling (ed.), *Die Evangelischen Kirchenordnung des XVI Jahrhunderts* 8 (Tübingen: J. B. Mohr, 1957): 104. English translation in Repp, *Confirmation*, p. 32.
21. Repp, *Confirmation*, p. 32.
22. Sehling, *Evangelischen Kirchenordnung* 8: 124. English translation in Fisher, *Christian Initiation: The Reformation Period*, p. 180.
23. Quoted in Fisher, *Christian Initiation: The Reformation Period*, p. 57.
24. *Ibid.*, p. 64.
25. *Ibid.*, p. 195.
26. Jean Calvin, *Institutes of the Christian Religion*, ed. J. T. McNeill, trans. F. L. Battles, Library of the Christian Classics 21 (Philadelphia: Westminster Press, 1960): 1460.
27. *Ibid.*, p. 1451.
28. S. L. Ollard, "Confirmation in the Anglican Communion," *Confirmation or the Laying on of Hands* 1 (New York: Macmillan, 1926): 62f.
29. F. E. Brightman, *The English Rite* 2 (London: Rivingtons, 1915): 776 (spelling modernized).
30. Fisher, *Christian Initiation: The Reformation Period*, p. 249; see also E. C. Whitaker, *Martin Bucer and the Book of Common Prayer*, Alcuin Club Collections 55 (Great Wakering: Mayhew-McCrimmon, 1974): 113.
31. George H. Williams (ed.), *The Radical Reformation* (Philadelphia: Westminister Press, 1962): 300–319. See also Rollin S. Armour, *Anabaptist Baptism*, Studies in Anabaptist and Mennonite History 11 (Scottdale, Pennsylvania: Herald Press, 1966).
32. Williams, *Radical Reformation*, pp. 120–123.
33. Armour, *Anabaptist Baptism*, p. 123.
34. *Ibid.*, p. 143.
35. *Ibid.*, p. 55.
36. *Ibid.*, p. 144.
37. *Ibid.*, p. 132.
38. Williams, *Radical Reformation*.
39. Luther's First and Second *Taufbuchlein*, Zwingli's two orders of baptism, The 1st and 2nd Prayer Books of Edward VI. All are in Fisher, *Christian Initiation: The Reformation Period*.
40. David G. Perrey, *Baptism at 21* (New York: Vantage Press, 1973). Aidan Kavanagh, "The Norm of Baptism: The New Rite of Christian Initiation of Adults," *Worship* 48 (1974): 143–152.

CHAPTER V

Christian Initiation:
Post-Reformation to the Present Era

Daniel B. Stevick

AS HE MINISTERS THE INITIATORY RITES, EVERY PASTOR IS THEOLOGIAN, teacher, and celebrant. But scholarship tends to divide this living material of concrete Christian experience. Liturgy, catechetics, and theology are studied and written about separately. It seems to me that much of the basic scholarly work on the manner of making Christians in the modern world remains to be done.

The available evidence might not, even under the most diligent study, tell us more than a part of what we would like to know. How did pastors, who were not leaders and who did not write books, teach? How methodically was confirmation observed in those generations for which episcopal and parochial records have not been given scholarly examination? Often one assumes that ways to which we are accustomed have always been followed in our traditions; attention needs to be given to the extent to which our present familiar practices have been shaped by the nineteenth century. What did the hundreds of thousands of ordinary Christians think that baptism meant as they observed it from generation to generation? What was said and done in the baptismal ceremonies in those churches that had no written liturgies?

A serious difficulty stems from the division of the churches of the modern West. Patterns of Christian initiation have developed independently, and few of us are conversant with many parts of this fragmented story. All I shall try to do with such elusive and scattered material is to start a few probes of moments and people, giving special attention to the interaction of catechetical practice and theological motifs with liturgy.

The prevailing pattern—the Roman community and the major

traditions of the Reformation, that is, Lutheran, Reformed, and Anglican—continued a two-stage rite of initiation which had become characteristic in the West since the late Middle Ages. By virtually universal practice, baptism was a rite performed within a few days of a child's birth. It was theologically the more important of the two stages; it signified and conveyed the redemptive reality. The second stage, admission to communion, usually followed some public confirmation rite and had become associated with a later period of life when one comes of age, takes one's place in the world, arrives at some competence and understanding. The Church groups which continued the two-stage pattern were not in full agreement since their theologies and practices were governed by distinct ideas, and varying accounts were given of each of the stages of initiation and of the relationship between them. Terms such as *grace, covenant, calling, regeneration, sealing,* and the *Spirit,* were all matters of dispute.

Considering all these groups together perhaps is not perfectly accurate, yet it is somewhat justified inasmuch as this initiatory pattern would, as it was lived, provide for each Christian a similar sequence of events. Since baptism was administered in infancy, the meaning and pledge of that baptism had to develop later. Baptism was followed by catechesis or, to put it the other way, catechesis was something provided for a baptized child. Through teaching, it was hoped that the divine life efficaciously signified in baptism would grow into responsible, godly living. At least that was the ideal, and strenuous efforts were put forth to make it work.

The sixteenth century was a time of educational creativity and, in order to make learning generally available, both Luther and Calvin exerted themselves strongly in behalf of schools. Luther's *Letter to the Mayors and Aldermen of All the Cities of Germany in Behalf of Christian Schools* is a landmark in the history of education. The Counter-Reformation saw the emergence of other great educational foundations such as the Confraternity of Christian Doctrine, and the work of Ignatius Loyola, and Charles Borromeo.

Within the specifically ecclesiastical life of the sixteenth century, catechisms proliferated. The term "catechism" seems to have been coined by Luther. The Reformation impulse stressed faith as *ficucia:* true faith was not consent to authoritative teaching, but a personal trust in the living God. Since it depended on hearing the Word of God, a popular knowledge of the Scriptures was necessary. The very character of faith itself required that it be expressed in word and in the ordering of life. The catechism was a handy device for imparting basic instruction in the meaning of life under God. Jungmann thinks that it was in response to the effectiveness of Luther's work that the Roman community recognized the need for written documents of Christian instruction.[1]

Some catechisms were lengthy and were meant as handbooks for the clergy to use in their catechizing work. Luther's *Large Catechism* (1529) was of this sort. The first of three catechisms by Peter Canisius (issued 1555) was on the grand scale: *Summa doctrinae christianae*. Of course, the catechism of the Council of Trent (1566), which influenced Catholicism for so long, was intended for pastors.

Other catechisms were shorter, more simple and direct, and were meant to be learned by lay Christians, usually children. Luther's *Small Catechism* was a highly successful work of this kind.

Several catechisms of the sixteenth and seventeenth centuries became classics of their languages and cultures. Luther's two catechisms are among his finest works. The *Heidelberg Catechism* (1563) is a minor masterpiece. In the Church of England, a small, rather pedestrian catechism appeared in the successive editions of the *Book of Common Prayer,* printed between the baptism and the confirmation services. But the Dean of St. Paul's, Alexander Nowell, prepared a more adequate catechism (written in 1562 but officially approved only in 1570, after many revisions). Until it was supplanted by the *Westminster Catechism* in 1647, Nowell's Catechism saw more than forty editions. After the Restoration, it was again in great demand.[2]

In some parts of the church, catechizing was apparently expected to be largely the responsibility of families, especially the parents. Inevitably, however, much of the responsibility for teaching fell to the clergy. The Council of Trent demanded that "the children in every parish be carefully taught the rudiments of faith and obedience toward God and their parents by those whose duty it is."[3] In many communities, Sunday afternoons were devoted to teaching both adults and children.

A rubric in the *Book of Common Prayer* stipulated:

> The Curate of every Parish shall diligently upon Sundays and Holy-days, after the Second Lesson at Evening Prayer openly in the Church instruct, and examine so many children of his parish sent unto him as he shall think convenient in some part of this Catechism.[4]

If the children were to be sent to the curate for teaching and examination, the rubric specifies also the duty of those who were to do the sending:

> And all fathers, Mothers, Masters, and Dames, shall cause their children, servants, and Prentices (which have not learned their catechism) to come to the Church at the time appointed, and obediently to hear, and be ordered by the Curate, until such time as they have learned all that is here appointed for them to learn.

This, however, was not the end of the matter, for canon 59 of the Canons of 1604 enjoins that if any minister neglect his duty to catechize, he is to be reproved and reported to the bishop after the first complaint. After a second offense, he could be suspended. And "if so the third time, there being little hope that he will be therein reformed, then excommunicated, and so remain until he will be reformed."[5]

It is difficult to infer what was really going on in the church to necessitate such laws. Perhaps these laws were written by leaders who earnestly sought to raise standards of pastoral responsibility, although such laws also reveal a situation of long-standing incompetence and neglect which some hierarchs thought could be dealt with by compulsion and threats. We admit today that good Christian teaching is an event within the church in response to the gospel, that it occurs where the finger of God touches the community and faith speaks to faith. Ignorance and carelessness cannot be overcome by ecclesiastical regulation alone.

As to the content of the teaching, most of the sixteenth and seventeenth-century catechisms of all denominations were solid works of instruction, organized around classic units of the creed, the Lord's Prayer, and the ten commandments. Although polemics (anti-Roman or anti-Protestant) were present, they were minimal. Each catechism, of course, had the marks of its own author or tradition. Luther, for example, put the ten commandments first and used them for a soteriological rather than an ethical point. The function of the commandments was not a guide for life, but rather a declaration of the divine law with which we struggle and against which our inadequacy is demonstrated, thus directing us to the gospel.

In a long essay on the Reformed catechisms, T. F. Torrance identifies a change in tone between the earlier and the later catechetical writings.[6] The earlier tend to be more what we might today call existential. They express a living religion, a direct sense of God's demand, of grace, and of the confidence of life in relation to God. The *Heidelberg Catechism* (1563) begins movingly:

Q.1: What is your only comfort in life and in death?

Ans.: That I, with body and soul, both in life and in death, am not my own, but belong to my faithful Savior Jesus Christ. . . .

The later catechisms were more abstract. *The Westminster Larger Catechism* (1648) provides an example. After referring the inquirer to the Holy Scriptures as the source for knowledge of God, the catechism asks:

Q.6: What do the Scriptures make known of God?

Ans.: The Scriptures make known what God is, the persons in the Godhead, His decrees, and the execution of His decrees.

Here an external authority is identified, its teachings are set down, categories and distinctions come in early, concrete experience comes late, as deduction from general principles. The scholastic temper has settled over the churches of the Reformation. Indeed, until quite recently, catechetical literature has shown a fondness for lists and formal parallels—the seven kinds of "this" or the three purposes of "that." Such patterned things can be easily memorized, of course, and verbal mastery of them can be verified. But such a method labors the derivative formulation, hoping to recreate the original insight. It can be like trying to explain music criticism to someone who is deaf.

Another problem with the catechism as a style of teaching is that one voice, the church, supplies both the questions and the answers. The form is dialogical, but no real dialogue takes place.

Torrance takes a high line in defense of this method.[7] He argues that material must be imparted in a way appropriate to its character. The Word of God, he says, does not answer the human questions. Rather, it tells us that we are asking the wrong questions. Hence, Christian faith is a matter of redefining the questions as well as of learning how they are to be answered. The catechetical form is, therefore, useful to tell us what we should be asking. There is, in my judgment, some validity to this line of thought, for our deepest questions and our most satisfying answers tend to mirror one another. The Christian message does uncover in us questions and needs of which we might otherwise be unaware. No catechism, however, ever expressed just the Word of God—eternal and the same for all people in all ages. Any catechism is, in some degree, the essential Christian kerygma filtered through the insights and limitations imposed by the cultural and religious idiom of a given time and place. Its questions and answers are not universal, but culturally specific and time-bound. The human material is indefinitely rich, complex, plural, and changing. Inevitably, any instructional formulation which has provided the questions and the answers will become dated and localized. A generation eventually will arise which simply cannot recognize itself in the self-contained world of the catechism.

Within the first century and a half of the Reformed era the major traditions were consolidated as folk-churches of whole populations. Children were still baptized at birth, as had been the custom for centuries. The dominant churches influenced and controlled the educational systems. A literature for catechetics was available. After some instruction, and between the ages of seven and twelve, a child would be confirmed (by the bishop in episcopally ordered communions, by the pastor elsewhere) and admitted to the eucharist. In Roman Catholicism, confirmation was regarded primarily as a sacramental rite granting increased grace for adult life and service. In the Reformed churches it was thought of primarily as catechetical, preparing a child to make for himself the commitments made on his behalf by sponsors at his birth. These two ideas of confirmation were combined in Anglicanism. In any case, a child became a Christian by consenting to a pattern in the culture in which he grew up. As he came to terms with the values of society, he also came to terms with God and the church.

Since the sixteenth century, there have been those who looked at the manner of becoming a Christian in ways other than in this two-stage pattern. In the eyes of the Anabaptists and other radical reformers, the church is not a natural community living a continuous life from generation to generation. Certainly the church should be independent of the political order; it receives no legitimation from the state and cannot justly be controlled by the state. Rather, the church is called into being by the act and summons of God. This act is not just an historical founding; it is a fresh act, renewed in every age. The church is formed by believing persons freely coming together in mutual covenant in response to the call of God. Infant baptism had been a sign of the old organic conception of the church. The radical sectarian critique of ecclesiology broke with the pattern of infant baptism and introduced, with some painful awkwardness in the transition, "believer's baptism."[8]

Baptism, by this account, is a public act witnessing to one's faith and made in obedience to Christ. One is constituted a Christian by conscious faith. Baptism belongs not to the economy of salvation but to the economy of obedience. It is not something that is done for one by the Church as part of becoming a Christian; rather, it is something done by one who has already become a Christian by conversion. In such a context, true baptism is impossible for an infant. In terms of the above analysis, "believer's baptism" is not a two-stage initiatory rite; it has only a single stage, one that would correspond (in the case of a person brought up within a practicing Christian home) to the second stage of the two-stage pattern. Baptism must wait until a person can, on his own, give an account of faith; otherwise the rite becomes magical, a mechanization of grace.

This manner of becoming a Christian, in which baptism is seen as profession of actual faith, has seemed self-evidently right to many people in the modern era. Groups which practice believer's baptism are, of course, numerically very important in the individualistic religious community of the United States. They are no longer sectarians mounting a critique against a prevailing practice. They virtually constitute the state church of some regions. It may not be ungracious to suggest that in such a situation, the "believer's baptism" pattern, which could score points in opposition to infant baptism perfunctorily administered, has had time on its own to show some inadequacies.

The location of baptism exclusively within adulthood fails to interpret and support the place of the child in the church. I hope it is more than a debater's point to suggest that we have it on good authority that there is something normative in the life of the kingdom about a child. The adult is the odd one who must change and become like a child in order to enter. A system which seems to say, "Except you become as a grown-up, you shall in no wise enter . . ." at least does not have all of the arguments in its favor. Does God reach us only through conscious, rational processes? Can he deal with us savingly only as discrete, individual adults? Are there not pre-conscious materials, basic to the reasoned-out formulations, which bind together Christian with Christian and elders with children in the life in Christ? In some Baptist communities the significance of childhood in the church is increasingly recognized by having children baptized at quite an early age. Some rigorist Baptists, however, oppose this development, thinking it compromises the adult character of the ordinance. In modern society, whether baptism is administered at age five or six or twelve or thirteen, it comes well before a person is socially or emotionally on his own. Any adolescent baptism is still so controlled by the expectations of the elder generation (internalized by the child) that it is hardly distinctively adult in character. In fact, the usual practice of believer's baptism is sometimes psychologically or sociologically more like deferred infant baptism.

In some Baptist communities, a dedication service gives recognition to a first stage. And of course, Baptist parents do not treat their children as exiles from Christ and from grace until they come to adult faith. But godly parental impulse needs to be supported, interpreted, and directed by theology, a theology of the child in the church which, in Baptist circles, appears quite faint.

It may be evident that the account and the customs of becoming a Christian have, in the modern West, developed around a dialectic of spirit versus structure, individual conviction versus institutional conformity, inward faith versus external rite. In the great seventeenth century drive for reduction to essentials, it may have been inevitable that this dialectic would be pushed to its logical limit. If some groups could be accused of having the "merely external" rite without the inward experience, someone would eventually claim the inward reality apart from any sacramental sign. The Society of Friends questioned not two sacramental steps in favor of having only one; it questioned sacraments altogether. The Quakers lived in a baptized society in which many persons had the external sign of baptism but showed little evidence of Christlikeness. They contended that the inward spirituality, of which the sacraments were intended to speak, is the constitutive thing in religious life. As long as one can have this inward reality directly, apart from rites, what use are the rites? They can add nothing to what is apprehended as a self-imparting of God himself to us.

Perhaps with respect to the ritual structures of initiation, these patterns—the two-stage, the one-stage, and the no-stage—define the possibilities with which the churches of the West have worked. Some explorations of ways of faith have counterpointed these sacramental structures and are informative.

The Puritan tradition provides one fascinating moment. Calvin had spoken of the church as a baptized community in which the Word was truly preached and the sacraments rightly administered, and he sought courageous and articulate faith on the part of Christians. He had not, however, thought of anything as constituting a test of membership. The English Puritan movement began by preaching, teaching, and exercising discipline. In the society of the time, everyone was baptized, but few were serious about faith or holiness. The Puritans sought an instructed, disciplined level of Christian life. Some of them, especially in New England, went beyond Calvin by making church membership conditional upon evidence of saving faith. The church should be a visible company of saints.[9] The Puritans baptized their children, recalling the promise that the covenant was "to you and to your children." The family was a school of piety; the Bible was read and the catechism taught; emphasis was placed on children. But each person had to look within himself for the signs of election. Emphasizing predestination as they did, salvation was regarded as so distinctly a work of God that it was legitimate to ask whether or not one might do anything to prepare for faith. The initial Puritan response was in the negative. Anything that a person might do towards his own salvation would compromise it as a work of God alone; it would elevate natural abilities and cheapen grace.[10] The saving relation with God lay in the mystery of his electing purpose. But in the Puritan community the idea gained ground that some preparedness for the work of grace was called for, even if it was the somewhat negative preparation of struggle with one's evil nature and conviction before God's law. On this point, Thomas Hooker wrote: "There is no faith can be infused into the soul before the heart be prepared. No preparation, no perfection. Never humbled, never exalted."[11] So a literature developed reflecting a style of self-examination, which emphasized the awakening from carelessness about one's condition, the recognition of the grip of sin, the readiness for the stirrings of the divine life within. When the signs of the work of God were clear, an unbeliever could be brought into the church, or a child could "own the covenant."

This feature of Puritanism suggested a respect for inward experience and a tendency to self-analysis which have remained marks of American Protestantism. It is also noteworthy that for some strains of Protestant thought, teaching itself could become a problem. For the Word of God confronts our perversity and our habit of sin. We cannot learn this Word in the way we can learn our history or arithmetic lessons; if we think we can, we are not really grasping it as Word of God. It can be preached, and preached so as to seek personal transformation, but the way of the Word, according to some styles of theology, does not lend itself to programs of teaching.

Another interesting feature occurs in the Pietist movement of the seventeenth century. Continental Protestantism had acquired the characteristics of a heavy, intellectualist orthodoxy. The battles of a century and a half left the traditions exhausted and defensive. The Pietist movement, led initially by Philip Spener (1635–1705), protested this lethargy in the name of inwardness and spiritual intensity.[12] Religion was a matter of the heart as well as of the head: *Den Kopf ins Herz zu bringen.* The Pietists worked in a largely Lutheran context in which nearly everyone was baptized, and they sought to bring about within this baptized population centers of conviction, fellowship, and service—*ecclesiolae* within the great, complacent *ecclesia.* Such communities were to be created by conversion. In the Lutheran tradition up to this point, confirmation had not developed uniformly. Luther himself had allowed for it, but had provided no liturgical text, no model for practice, and no authoritative rationale. The rite was not used at all in some parts of Lutheranism. Bucer had developed it quite fully, but his lead was not everywhere followed. To the Pietists confirmation seemed to be an unexploited pastoral opportunity, and, accordingly, they adopted it as a rite of conversion. Within their conversion theology, the Pietists emphasized confirmation as a solemn vow; it was to be not merely a consent to the church's formularies, but a witness to one's personal faith and a commitment to the obligation of Christian life. Such a use of the tradition of confirmation could easily slip into subjectivism and individualism, although some features of Pietist practice and understanding had wide and prolonged influence.

Not only within Pietism, however, but wherever Protestantism took its catechetical job seriously, it seems to have tended to promote confirmation as a rite of considerable importance. Confirmation was considered the culmination of a period of concentrated preparation and teaching and an occasion of religious crisis, decision-making, or public commitment. All of these were important in becoming a Christian, and all of these had been missing from baptism as usually practiced and understood.

Some theories of catechesis, as we have noted, regarded it as necessary that baptized persons be converted. Although they bear the sign of baptism, Christians needed to be awakened from sin and complacency and brought to real faith.

It should be noted, if somewhat parenthetically, that during this very same period the Roman communion began to communicate children before confirmation, and then to require a confession of sins prior to this first communion. The occasion of this first communion became surrounded by a heavy religious, emotional, and social investment, for the individual, the family, and the parish. I do not think it would be too hazardous to suspect that as initiatory rites which capture the genius of their communities, these two rites (confirmation among Protestants and first communion among Roman Catholics), with more recent generations, have, in popular awareness, come to surpass the importance of baptism.

One of the giants of educational thought was Johann Amos Comenius (1592–1670), a Moravian bishop, and a man of peace, who lived in a time of turmoil and spent much of his life as a refugee. His educational ideas apply to a general reform of schools, and they are largely contained in *The Great Didactic: Setting*

Forth the Whole Art of Teaching All Things to All Men (1632).
Comenius announces his educational intention:

> The Beginning and End of our Didactic will be: To seek and
> find a method by which the teachers teach less and the learners
> learn more, by which the schools have less noise, obstinacy, and
> frustrated endeavor, but more leisure, pleasantness, and definite
> progress, and by which the Christian State will suffer less under
> obscurity, confusion, and conflict, and will enjoy a greater
> amount of light, order, peace, and quiet.[13]

Education, Comenius held, was an urgent business because "the
salvation of the human race is at stake." His principles can be set
down briefly. Man is the most excellent of God's works, and his
ultimate end lies outside this life, in God. This life is a three-stage
preparation for eternity—to know the world and oneself, to rule
oneself, to direct oneself to God. "In these three things is situated
the whole excellence of man." The capacities for all three are
implanted in man, but must be developed by education. "Indeed, it
is only by education that one can become a man." The method of
teaching should thus follow nature and observe a due order. And
Nature is gradual, working from within, adapting means to ends,
relating part to part intelligibly. Freed from coercion, education
should thus unfold naturally, cooperating with the manner of
human growth. "As in other matters, so in this; where God
supplies means, to ask for a miracle is to tempt him."[14]

Comenius stressed human capacities and destiny rather than
human sin. There is no suggestion in his thought that grace
contradicts nature. He thus had a sense of the distinctiveness of
childhood which made him, finally, a humane educational vision-
ary of great stature.

When we say that Comenius was ahead of his time, we are
probably congratulating ourselves by implying that we have caught
up with him, but we can note that ideas such as his had little
influence in the century and a half after they appeared. The
Christianity of the eighteenth century was heavy on rational
content and moral maxims. Childhood found little sympathy, and
was viewed "as a condition to be worked off with all due
speed."[15]

Isaac Watts, an eminent English Independent divine, was responsible for an important effort to write religious material expressly

for children. *Divine and Moral Songs for Children,* published in 1720, remained in print well into the last century and is, by any accounting, one of the world's all-time best sellers. A few lines may indicate the tone:

> Let dogs delight to bark and bite,
>   For God hath made them so.
> Let lions and tigers growl and fight,
>   For 'tis their nature too,

> But children, you should never let
>   Such angry passions rise.
> Your little hands were never made
>   To tear each other's eyes.[16]

Most of the voluminous work from the eighteenth and nineteenth centuries impresses us as having been writing not *for* children, but *at* children. Even when Watts puts some of his verses in the form of a child speaking, the voice is that of the adult world telling a child what to think and feel.

Only with Romanticism was the Western imagination able to sympathetically enter the mind and world of a child.[17] Blake wrote the first convincing poetry in a child's self and voice. Rousseau's *Emile* took the side of the child. Pestalozzi's educational intuitions, at this same time, opened possibilities for an emancipated childhood.

At first this new awareness of the child did the church little good. In the novels of Charles Dickens and of Charlotte Brontë, parsons rank alongside parents (perhaps more commonly stepparents) and schoolmasters in a triumvirate of wicked oppressors of children. The Romantics who identified with the child (often enough with the child as especially close to God) thought of the church as an enemy.

Eventually the new insights about childhood and human community found their way into some Christian thinking where they could bring about change in the ways of religious teaching. The great New England Congregationalist, Horace Bushnell issued his important book *Christian Nurture* in 1847. He opposed the revivalistic idea, which seemed to teach that in a scheme of mercy for mankind, God had appointed children to years of sin before they acquired the maturity for individual conversion. He felt that the family was an organic community through which the character, feelings, spirit, and principles of the parents would inevitably pass to the children in ways more pervasive and subtle than direct teaching, persuading, or governing. "Your spirit is to pass into them, by a law of transition that is natural and well nigh irresistable."[18] His classic proposition was: "That the child is to grow up a Christian, and never know himself as being otherwise."[19] Bushnell's ideas pioneered the approach to religious education which seeks to cooperate with the developing experience of a child in a Christian family and congregation.

I have left out more than I have told, but the basic material is before us. Within the twentieth century, much has been done in developmental psychology; we have observational detail and interpretive categories never before available. Social changes have altered family structure and ways of growing up. But the moral, religious, and humanistic values with which we now work represent fresh trading with some of the long-held capital of the West.

General Observations

The above account is only a fragment of the story of the ways to Christ in the modern world. The material might have been organized quite differently. I have set it down so as to emphasize differences. It is important to realize that all these varieties are parts of one history. All of our clumsy attempts to bring persons to the fold of the True Shepherd are manifestations of that "one baptism" which we affirm in the creed, and which is Christ's own gift. But more traceably, all have emerged in a common history which often protests in the name of some important insight, sometimes overcorrecting, sometimes grasping a neglected *desideratum* at the cost of ignoring something else. All of our ways of Christian initiation judge one another, and each needs judgment on itself. The crisis of church life in which we live has therefore brought up for review the received wisdom of four hundred years. And because the life in Christ is an infinitely rich and mysterious experience, no rite or doctrine has caught that reality finally or definitively. We need however to be open to the past for the sake of openness to the future.

From the account sketched above, six factors have been emphasized, singly or in combinations:

1. The Church: one becomes a Christian by identification, through the instituted rite of death and rebirth, with the world- and time-embracing people of Christ.
2. The family: one becomes a Christian in the embrace of a social unit which is an agent of God's creative and redemptive purpose.
3. Teaching: one becomes a Christian through internalizing the witness of faith to the character and acts of God.
4. Gradual development: one grows in his relation with God as one fulfills his human potential.
5. Conversion: one becomes a Christian in a deliberate act of forsaking sin and confessing Christ as Savior and Lord.
6. The Spirit: none of the above is automatic. Becoming a Christian is in the mystery of the Spirit's work. We can set sails, but we cannot make the wind blow. The signs of faith are given and withheld unexpectedly.

All of these factors are valuable; they belong to one another. But they have become separate as though individually they were property of churches, or movements, or schools of thought.

In isolation emphases can develop undesirable side effects. The stress, both on the institution and on the *given* factors of becoming a Christian, tend not to define the life of adult faith into which a child will move. Rather it delimits the heavy-handed system against which one tests oneself and away from which one often turns in the course of self-fulfillment. The family has been overdiscovered several times. Emphasis on *credenda* in the initiatory process can intellectualize the gospel and put a premium on mastery of a Christian gnosis. Gradual personal development can, as an isolated factor, minimize the radical claim of the gospel and the weight of sin. The twice-born, conversionist emphases create intense but elitist communities of like-minded people. For the wholeness of the gospel and of life, we need to transcend our broken past.

In the historical material presented above, I have emphasized many non-ritual factors because the sacramental structures of the churches have been fairly constant for most of the modern era. Until quite recently, Roman Catholics, Lutherans, Anglicans, Baptists, and others were doing, saying, and meaning at baptism what they did, said, and meant in the formative generations of the modern era. What changes have taken place in the liturgies of Christian initiation have been relatively minor and uninteresting. The interest, the movement, the recountable history has been elsewhere. The durable ritual structures have experienced changes in theologies, educational theories, community forms, and the like as the great Christian traditions have participated (usually by responding to initiatives from the outside) in the free, individualistic, self-aware, rapidly changing culture of the West. The meaning of becoming a Christian has been influenced by rationalism, romanticism, the rise of psychology, the reshaping of society and the sensibility to industrialism and technology, and, above all, by the general de-Christianization of the West.

We are at the end of an era. The ritual forms themselves no longer seem to be doing their work. The two-stage rite is being questioned and scrutinized by its own children and heirs.

This two-stage rite was the creation of Western Christendom. By it a person was progressively initiated into the full life of the religious community. Everyone was a Christian by birth and infant baptism. The all-pervasive reality of Christian culture could provide continuity from this early introduction on to confirmation, to communicant status, and, indeed, to a life-time which was supported by a sacramental system ritualizing a theistic interpretation of life. Birth and the age of reason and responsibility might come at separated moments, but they were threaded together. One might grow into these stages as he grew into life itself.

But today Christian culture is not a close, tangible reality, which supports and interprets liturgy. We cannot count on everyday life to do our work for us.[20] The drift of modern, secularized culture will not carry anyone to Christ, but rather in the opposite direction. The believing community, like its crucified Lord, finds itself "outside the gate." But perhaps that is the place of true power.

With the death of Christendom, the inherited liturgy of Christian initiation has come to appear as a series of isolated ritual events. Baptism, confirmation, and first communion have been left stranded by the receding tide of faith. They are three moments with little obvious connection with one another and providing little sense of the whole of which they are parts.

When baptism is only a first stage which admits one to only a qualified participation in church life, it is a diminished sacrament. As long as something essential remains to be granted by some later stage of this progressive initiation, we seem to be saying that by baptism we are only partially related to God. If baptism requires something later as its "completion," we imply that it is incomplete. Someone who is not yet confirmed and not yet a communicant is "merely baptized." An ironic idea! Imagine trying to explain to St. Paul the status of someone who was "merely baptized." Confirmation has had two kinds of meanings associated with it in the Western tradition. The first group includes the rather accidental medieval meanings about growth and increase of grace. These interpretations appeared after the rite had been separated from infant baptism and set within a subsequent period of life. (I am assuming that the Reformation meanings of responsibility and confessing the faith could utilize the rite because the pre-Reformation interpretation turned in this direction.) The other class of meanings—gifts of the Spirit, priesthood, anointing, sealing, spiritual combat, commitment to the world, and many others—*are all baptismal meanings.* If they are associated in any exclusive way with confirmation, baptism is deprived of them. If they are shared by the two rites, they duplicate one another. The unity and decisiveness of baptism becomes qualified. As a sacramental rite, confirmation makes sense only in close association with the baptismal action. It cannot gather independent meanings around itself: it has no independent meanings. As regards first communion, it should be noted that the Church makes a person a member of Christ and the church by baptism, but immediately suspends him from the normal sacramental practice of Christian life. When the Church later lifts the suspension and admits that person to the eucharist, it allows the occasion to take on a festal air of doubtful appropriateness.[21] First communion is not an unrepeated observance, like ordination, marriage, or baptism. Rather it is an often repeated action to which one is properly admitted by reason of being baptized, not by reason of some subsequent new sacramental beginning. In the churches which have kept the baptism-confirmation-communion sequence, confirmation—and to a great extent the catechesis leading to it—has been effective because communicant status stood waiting at the end of it all. Communion was a reward, a carrot held before one's nose that kept one going to all those classes.

In summary, the Churches have built questionable dynamics and motivations into the initiatory rites, and they have used poor arguments to show that it all made sense. It seems clear that theologically the sacramental parts of Christian initiation are not intelligible except as elements in an understandable unity standing for the indivisible whole of the redemptive mystery. It is psychologically self-defeating to try to associate one part of this initiatory unity with one stage of life, and other parts with other stages when no such staged-out meanings belong inherently to the rites themselves.

A basic reshaping of our initiatory rites has been under way for some time. An ecumenical consensus seems to be gathering about what that new shape ought to be. Probably the staged-out initiatory ritual which has marked the modern era of church life will not survive into the era that is succeeding it.

NOTES

1. J. A. Jungmann, *Handing on the Faith: A Manual of Catechetics*, trans. A. N. Fuerst (New York: Herder and Herder, 1959): 20.

2. John R. Mulder, *The Temple of the Mind: Education and Literary Taste in Seventeenth Century England* (New York: Pegasus, 1969) has interesting material on Nowell and his work in chapter five and elsewhere throughout the book.

3. *Sess. XXIV de ref.*, c.4. (Schröder, ed.).

4. Versions of this rubric appeared in all the sixteenth and seventeenth century prayer book editions. It is quoted here from the text of 1661.

5. *The Constitutions and Canons Ecclesiastical of the Church of England*, 59. S. L. Ollard, "Confirmation in the Anglican Communion," *Confirmation or the Laying on of Hands* I (London: S.P.C.K., 1926): 60–245 gives extensive material on the efforts to enforce pastoral diligence in this period.

6. Thomas F. Torrance, *The School of Faith: The Catechisms of the Reformed Church* (New York: Harper & Brothers, 1959): xvi. ff.

7. *Ibid.*, pp. xxv. ff.

8. The best short historical account is probably W. M. S. West, "The Anabaptists and the Rise of the Baptist Movement," *Christian Baptism*, ed. A. Gilmore (Philadelphia: The Judson Press, 1959):223–272.

9. Edmund S. Morgan, *Visible Saints: The History of a Puritan Idea* (Ithaca: Cornell University Press, 1965), and the same author's *The Puritan Family: Religion and Domestic Relations in Seventeenth-Century New England* (New York: Harper Torchbooks, 1966).

10. Norman Pettit, *The Heart Prepared: Grace and Conversion in Puritan Spiritual Life* (New Haven: Yale University Press, 1966): 19.

11. Quoted in *ibid.*, p. 96.

12. See the summary in Arthur C. Repp, *Confirmation in the Lutheran Church* (Saint Louis: Concordia, 1964): 68–76.

13. Quoted in Robert Ulich (ed.), *Three Thousand Years of Educational Wisdom* (Cambridge: Harvard University Press, 1957): 340. The other citations of Comenius are from the 1896 translation by Keatinge.

14. *Ibid.*, passim.

15. Joseph F. Kett, "Adolescence and Youth in Nineteenth-Century America," *The Family in History*, eds. T. K. Rabb and R. I. Rotberg (New York: Harper Torchbooks, 1973): 99.

16. Isaac Watts, *Works* IV (1810 ed.): 397. These lines are from Song 16, "Against Quarrelling and Fighting." Other titles are, "Examples of Early Piety," "Solemn Thoughts of God and Death," "Against Idleness and Mischief," and "Obedience to Parents."

17. On this whole development of sensibility see Peter Coveney, *The Image of Childhood* (Baltimore: Penguin Books, 1967).

18. 1904 edition, p. 64.

19. *Ibid.*, p. 10. The volume as usually cited was published in 1861, but it gathered up previously published writings on the subject, including the small work of 1847 whose title was given also to the larger collection. Bushnell was an important theologian, but the theological content of *Christian Nurture* seems thin. Robert Ulich in *A History of Religious Education* (New York: New York University Press, 1968): 247 comments: "There prevails in *Christian Nurture* a monistic optimism with regard to the nature of childhood and the possibilities of Christian preparation inherent in a pious family. It represents the best of the American middle-class spirit with its belief in the reforming powers of good men; it is a book of a humanist grounded in a religious conception of the unity of the universe."

20. See the comment with which Juan Luis Segundo opens his *Grace and the Human Condition*, trans. John Drury, (Maryknoll, New York: Orbis Books, 1973): 3, "In the modern world no environment can give us Christianity ready-made. If what we possess has been handed over to us in this fashion, then we have good reason to believe that it is not truly Christianity at all but rather an oversimplified substitute."

21. Jungmann, *Handing on the Faith*, pp. 325f.

CHAPTER VI

Christian Initiation of Adults: The Rites

Aidan Kavanagh, OSB

THE *ORDO INITIATIONIS CHRISTIANAE ADULTORUM,*[1] PUBLISHED BY THE Sacred Congregation for Divine Worship in January of 1972,[2] is the last in a sequence of reforms in Roman Catholic initiatory polity that have altered the baptism of infants (1969) and the manner of confirmation by bishops (1971). The present *Ordo* is a document of 185 pages that, in addition to the full rites of adult initiation, contains a simpler form of the same rites for use in exceptional circumstances and a brief form to be used in peril of death. The following are also provided: rites preparatory to confirmation and first eucharist for adults who were baptized as infants but never received adequate catechesis at a later age; an order of initiation for children of older age who were never baptized as infants; and, in the appendix, an order of admission into full communion with the Roman Catholic Church for those who have already been validly baptized in another communion.

Here I shall limit my comments to the full rites of adult initiation contained in the first chapter of the *Ordo* (nos. 68–239), together with the introductory paragraphs relative to the full rites of adult initiation (1–67). The document is too lengthy as a whole to be treated adequately in an essay of this length. More importantly, however, it is my opinion[3] that in the full rites of adult initiation we have in fact the definitive exposition of what the Roman Catholic *norm of baptism* is henceforth to be. Because of this, the spirit and principles contained in the full rites of adult initiation will be found operative in the other rites contained in the document.

Concentrating on the full rites of adult initiation is advisable on

118

another, more strategic account as well. In the sheer quantity of ceremonial reforms that have issued forth during the past decade it is easy to miss what has been simultaneously occurring beneath the surface. The entire sacramental economy has received a radical redefinition and refurbishing that renders it a more influential paradigm for church order on the local level—a church order that can serve as focus for new theological reflection and as a structure for the renewal of Christian life in common. The previous separateness of the several sacraments has been compromised in a salutary manner by norms which regard the sacraments as closely articulated phases of a whole people's continuing life together in faith. Less do these same norms present the sacraments as discrete events geared to phases in an individual's life than as stages in the process of ecclesial living together under the aegis of Jesus Christ dying and rising continually among his faithful ones. This newly recovered perspective throws into bold relief the abnormality of relatively recent sacramental practice, creates new possibilities and problems in pastoral endeavor, and suggests new points of departure for pastoral, liturgical, and theological development.

The importance of the new *Ordo* stems, therefore, not so much from its ceremonial details as from its strategic vision of the church local and universal. Thus, it is less a document containing yet more ceremonial reforms than a practicable vision of what the church can become through that continuing renewal process known as Christian initiation. To the commission group that accomplished this work and to its chairman, Prof. Dr. Balthasar Fischer of the University of Trier, the church will likely be indebted for generations to come.[4]

The full rites for the initiation of adults include not only the closely articulated sacraments of baptism, confirmation, and eucharist (208–224) but also the rites of the catechumenate. Preceding these are ample explanations of the catechumenal phases of the initiation process (4–67). These preparatory explanations are not only welcome but also necessary, since by far the largest part of the initiatory sequence centers on the catechumenate (68–207). The catechumenate is here regarded not as a didactic or educative process but as an ecclesial and liturgical structure within which conversion therapy is carried on. Catechesis is understood to be concerned with conversion in Christ and with how to live continuously in such a manner not only prior to, but after, initiation as well. As such, far from being the exclusive domain of experts in religious education,

> The initiation of catechumens takes place step by step in the midst of the community of the faithful. Together with the catechumens, the faithful reflect upon the value of the paschal mystery, renew their own conversion, and by their example lead the catechumens to obey the Holy Spirit more generously (4).

That the initiation of catechumens takes place sequentially "in the midst of the community of the faithful" accounts for the several stages or steps being given a liturgical form and style. In this way, catechesis is no longer confined exclusively to classrooms but thrown open to the whole local church as a cycle of worship events that focus upon the critical issues of conversion in faith and renewal of life not only for individuals but for the entire ecclesial community as well. Catechumens are thus viewed not as anonymous attendants at private educational events known as inquiry classes, but as public persons in the local church whose faith, progress, and prognosis in communal faith-living are the concerns of the entire church met for solemn public worship of God. Catechesis and all it touches are less the preserve of "religious educators" than they are the right and "property" of the church of God.

Evangelization and Precatechumenate (9–13)

While the rite of initiation properly so-called begins formally with admission to the catechumenate, stages preliminary to this are regarded as critically important for what is to follow. These preliminary stages are referred to variously as a time for "making inquiry" and for investigation and maturation of purpose on the part of the seeker.

On the part of the local church this is a time of establishing trust and communication with the inquirer, of evangelizing the seeker by proclaiming ". . . the living God . . . and Jesus Christ, whom he sent for the salvation of all men" (9). By living well its own life of faith, the local church has not only attracted those of open hearts to itself but has also taken on obligations to such persons.

In this initial and preformal dialectic between inquirer and local church, a certain incipient but real communion with God through Christ in the Spirit has already been born. The solid theological reality of this communion, however potential and incipient it may yet be, stamps what follows with the mark of necessity rather than of vaguely recommended convenience. As seen in the *Ordo,* faith is not merely a benevolent disposition nor a sincere anguish over the state of the world and the elusiveness of truth. Faith is seen as a concrete commitment of one's soul and body to the society of those who know Jesus Christ, and him alone, to be "the way, the truth and the life."

The Catechumenate (14–20)

Only the foregoing gives grounds for the document to say that "The rite of becoming a catechumen is of very great importance" (14). It presupposes that the candidates for membership in the catechumenate are already grounded in the basics of " . . initial spiritual life and Christian teaching," a solid desire for ecclesial faith, and repentance together with a will to change one's life on entering into prayerful relationship with God in Christ among believing people (15). Assembling publicly before the local church for the first time, ". . . the candidates make their intention known to the Church; the Church, *carrying out its apostolic mission,* admits those who intend to become members" (14).[5] On admission, their names are inscribed in the register of catechumens (17), and henceforth the catechumens are regarded as Christians.[6]

Although not yet members of the faithful (this comes only with the initiatory sequence of baptism-confirmation-eucharist), catechumens occupy an overt place in church structure and discharge a real ministry to the church by witnessing in their own lives to the never-ending need of conversion in Christ that is requisite for the whole church, universal as well as local. What the restatement of this traditional principle will do to the convention of infant baptism remains to be seen, but it is likely that the latter will not remain unaffected by it indefinitely.

The catechumenate is ordinarily to last "several years," and its content is described in (19) as consisting in pastoral formation accomplished through "suitable discipline." What is to be discerned in the catechumen during this period is not so much intellectual adequacy regarding concepts having to do with faith but maturation in those dispositions toward the faith as a reality lived in common that were already manifest when the individual was admitted to the catechumenate. Aiding the maturation process is to be actively engaged in by the whole local church in four ways.

First, there is doctrinal formation by presbyters, deacons, catechists, and other professionally competent lay persons to enable the catechumens to attain a "... suitable knowledge of dogmas and precepts" and an "... intimate understanding of the mystery of salvation" (19.1). This formation is to be accommodated to the liturgical year and enriched by seasonal celebrations of the word, which implies that what is envisaged is not merely a classroom effort in watered-down "theology," but a well-rounded formation program that is suffused with a strong liturgical methodology. The document is clear on the purpose of catechesis: it is to form Christians who have something to repent of and celebrate, and who know how to do both in common.

Second, catechumens are to be formed by living closely with others who know well the demands and advantages of a Christian way of life. The exemplary role of sponsors, godparents, and the whole local community of faith is paramount in this mode of formation. One learns how to fast, pray, repent, celebrate, and serve the good of one's neighbor less by being lectured on these matters than by close association with people who do these things with regular ease and flair.

Third, and rather as a specification of the second way, the catechumens' regular participation in public worship eases them gently and over a considerable period of time into a sacramental way of life.

Ordinarily, however, when they are present in the assembly of the faithful, they should be dismissed in a friendly manner before the eucharistic celebration begins . . .; they must await their baptism, which will bring them into the priestly people and depute them to participate in the Christian worship of the New Covenant (19.3).

This means that while catechumens are regarded as Christians, their not yet being "of the faithful" should be manifested visibly in the worshiping assembly. The dismissal of catechumens before the Prayer of the Faithful and preparation of the gifts may in addition serve as an effective nonverbal catechesis for the faithful on the awesome dignity of their own baptism. To emphasize the real importance of this act it will be necessary to evolve some ritual form of dismissal, perhaps the community prayer for the catechumens, once again in the Roman Rite.[7]

Fourth, and finally, "Since the Church's life is apostolic, catechumens should also learn how to work actively with others to spread the Gospel and build up the Church by the testimony of their lives and the profession of their faith" (19.4). From this it is obvious that catechesis, in the sense of the document, goes quite beyond the classroom and its instructional techniques. What is envisaged here is not only formal "religious education" but an ecclesiology of social action in evangelization and in the corporal and spiritual acts of mercy. I suspect that the effects of such a program may well be at least as telling on the local church as on the catechumens.

The section on the catechumenate concludes by noting that, in something as long-term, complex, and demanding as this, nothing can be determined a priori (20). The adequacy of a catechumenate as regards both the catechumens and the local church to which they belong depends not on static guidelines to policy but on the wisdom and integrity of those responsible for setting the period of time and directing the discipline of the catechumenate. Those responsible in this case are said to be the bishop and, more generally, the episcopal conferences of the various nations.

Period of Purification and Enlightenment (21–26)

When it appears to the satisfaction of all those immediately concerned (local clergy, catechists, sponsors, and godparents) that a catechumen has attained by grace and effort a conversion of mind and life, a sufficient knowledge of Christian teaching, and a becoming sense of faith and charity, he or she may be "elected" by the local church to enter proximate preparation for the sacraments of initiation when next these are to be celebrated (22–24). The period of preparation is called a time of purification and enlightenment (21); it is described as a period of spiritual recollection more than catechesis and is intended to "purify minds and hearts by the examination of conscience and by repentance and also to enlighten by a deeper knowledge of Christ the Saviour" (25). This time coincides usually, if not always, with Lent—a season which, in its ethos, liturgy, and choice of readings, prepares for initiation on Holy Saturday and for reconciliation of penitents on Holy Thursday and Good Friday.

The liturgical structure given to the period of purification and enlightenment is very explicit in the document. The act of electing catechumens for sacramental initiation is said to belong to the whole local church, and it is to be done publicly after the homily at the main eucharistic celebration on the first Sunday in Lent (22, 139). The elect are then publicly scrutinized on their intentions and exorcised[8] after the homily at the main eucharistic celebrations on the third, fourth, and fifth Sundays in Lent. They are also formally presented with the creed and the Lord's Prayer at public celebrations during weekdays late in Lent, being expected to "give each back" by publicly reciting them at a later service (25.1 and 2).

On Holy Saturday the elect are instructed to rest from ordinary work if possible and to spend their time in prayer, recollection, and fasting. If there is a meeting of the elect that same day, some of the preparatory rites may be done—such as the profession of faith (the Nicene or Apostles' Creed), the *ephpheta* ceremony, the choosing of a Christian name (if this is customary), and the first anointing with the oil of catechumens.

The Sacraments of Initiation (27–36)

The sacraments of baptism, confirmation, and the eucharist together constitute

> . . . the final stage in which the elect come forward and, with their sins forgiven, are admitted into the people of God, receive the adoption of the sons of God and are led by the Holy Spirit into the promised fullness of time and, in the eucharistic sacrifice and meal, to the banquet of the Kingdom of God (27).

While the document presupposes that all this will be done normally within the liturgy of the Easter vigil (208), it notes that even when it takes place at some other time of the year ". . . the celebration should be filled with the Easter spirit" (209).

The insistence on the Easter vigil as the *normative* setting for Christian initiation is neither ecclesiastical nostalgia nor doctrinal wistfulness. There is simply no other time of the year, and certainly no other liturgical context, that so splendidly serves as a setting for sacramental initiation and its meaning. Not only are the initiates dying and rising in Christ as the church commemorates his passage from death to life long ago; more importantly, the initiates are entering into his corporate real presence in the universe, the church, where his passage from death and "this world" to life unbounded remains an ongoing reality that is the pivot on which the renewed cosmos turns. Only the Easter vigil yields up an ecclesiology that is worthy of baptism. The constant separation of baptism from this paschal context heretofore has weakened our theology both of the church and of Christian initiation—to the detriment of the church's self-understanding, of the faithful Christian's own sense of his or her individual identity, and of the church's mission in the world.

When the Easter vigil "speaks" about initiation, it does so in terms of a veritable evangelization of the cosmos. Fire, wind, wax, bees, light and darkness, water, oil, nakedness, bread, wine, aromas, tough and graceful words and gestures: all these stand as a context without which what happens to one entering corporate faith in Jesus Christ dead and rising is only partially perceptible. The being and acts of Christ himself can even become constricted without regular paschal access to the full sweep of God's purpose that was being revealed long before the incarnation occurred.[9] Because the discipline of Christian initiation is impoverished without regular access to the full paschal sweep of God's intents and accomplishment in Jesus Christ, the church becomes less than it is and may be, and so does the world. And what greater calamity can fall upon the church than the loss of Easter? What Emerson said about the loss of worship can here be applied to Easter.

Then all things go to decay. Genius leaves the temple to haunt the senate or the market. Literature becomes frivolous. Science is cold. The eye of the baptized is not lighted by the hope of other worlds, and age is without honor. The Church lives to trifles, and when men die we do not mention them.[10]

Some words are needed on the document's plan for the sacraments of initiation within the Easter vigil. After the homily, the ministers, the elect, and their godparents go to the font or baptistry where an exhortation is given by the presiding minister and the litany of the saints is sung. Then the following order is observed:

1. Blessing of baptismal water (215–216)
2. Renunciation of evil (217)
3. Anointing with the oil of catechumens if this has not already been done (218)
4. Profession of faith (219)
5. Baptism by immersion or infusion (220–222)
6. Anointing with chrism *if* confirmation is deferred for some special reason (223–224)
7. Giving a white garment and candle (225–226)
8. Confirmation (227–231)
9. The paschal eucharist, beginning with the preparation of the gifts (232–234)

Several matters deserve comment. First, the order of sacramental initiation's placement after the homily and before the first eucharist of Easter day in reality makes all that precedes it an extensive pre-eucharistic synaxis of the word that centers upon the candidates for baptism. The synaxis of the word may thus tend to have more the character of a "theme mass" for the candidates, rather as funerals seem to be taking on a thematic emphasis centering on the deceased's life. This is a mistake at least in emphasis. Neither the vigil nor a funeral (nor for that matter a wedding or an ordination) is a liturgy "for" someone. They are celebrations *of* the church, *by* the church, and *for* the church under the criteria of the gospel. Keeping this in mind and developing a sense of reticent reverence with regard to what must be said and what really should not be said, might keep liturgical events more robustly large, thus allowing more of those present to participate better instead of feeling "shut out" from an event that has become too personally oriented and tactical in scope.

The placement of initiation after the homily, furthermore, may also force the synaxis of the word to take on more the character of the candidates' final catechetical session than that of a true vigil of watch and prayer. Early historical evidence suggests to me that the vigil of Easter was more strictly just that—a *vigil* of watch and prayer in which readings were employed not to instruct the elect about baptism but to galvanize the faithful in their intense wait for the Mother of Feasts to begin. The vigil may well have even been carried on by the *fideles* while the elect were being baptized in a place separate from the vigil-assembly. Baptism *in camera* was then the rule due to the required nakedness of the candidates. This fact would almost necessitate some kind of formal presentation of the newly baptized, now anointed and dressed, to the assembly of faithful, who had been keeping vigil in the church while the baptisms were in progress. And it may be that the ritual demands of such a presentation of the neophytes to the faithful were responded to by the senior baptizing minister (usually the bishop) with a solemn imposition of hands, public prayer, and a final anointing with aromatic chrism done amidst the faithful and greeted by them with ovations. This may be the practical genesis of what would later be called confirmation.[11] The point is not a major one, but it might be kept in mind lest confirmation continue to be regarded as more separate a sacrament, and of more moment, than in fact it is.

A second matter is the reiterated recognition in the Roman Rite of baptism by immersion. "If baptism is by immersion of the whole body or of the head only, decency and decorum should prevail" (220). The rubrical concern for decency and decorum would not be necessary to state unless there were a practical regard for total or partial immersion being actually done. Baptizing this way would be a welcome development—welcome because it might help restore both something of the crucial and extraordinary nature of baptism to our consciousness, and some of the drastic robustness to baptismal symbolism, which for too long has been enfeebled by minimalism, privacy, and the anonymity of the baptized.

A third and most important matter is what is done with confirmation. The document is clear on the point that confirmation should normally happen immediately on baptism and within the same liturgical event. "According to the ancient practice maintained in the Roman liturgy, an adult is not to be baptized unless he receives confirmation immediately afterward, provided no serious obstacles exist. *This connection signifies the unity of the paschal mystery, the close relationship between the mission of the Son and the pouring out of the Holy Spirit, and the joint celebration of the sacraments by which the Son and the Spirit come with the Father upon those who are baptized"* (34; emphasis added).

The theological point made here is of such seriousness that one feels compelled to ask why and how it can be construed as applying only to adults and not to infants and children, especially if they are baptized at the Easter vigil. Unless the theological point is dismissed as mere rhetoric, it seems inescapable that all who are deemed fit for baptism, no matter what their physical age, should also be confirmed within the same liturgical event. This seems to have in fact been the discipline in the Roman Church until the Early Middle Ages, and it is still the practice of the Orthodox Churches. The continued Western practice of deferring confirmation of infants and children, more recently even until adolescence, will have to take account of the theological principle stated clearly in (34), a principle that would require construal of physical age as "a serious obstacle" to sacramental reception. But if this is proved, then it is inevitable that the same question be posed about baptism of infants: if age is a serious obstacle to receiving confirmation, why then is age not a serious obstacle to receiving baptism? Theological discussion will have to cope with this anomaly.

While bishops, to whose office confirmation has been closely restricted in the Roman Rite, are urged to preside at the Lenten catechumenal liturgies, to celebrate the rite of election, and to preside at the sacraments of initiation during the Easter vigil (44), their necessary absence from the latter should not continue to force confirmation to be done quite apart from baptism and the eucharist. The document, therefore, opens the ministry of confirmation to any presbyter who has some diocesan function or office, is a pastor either of the place where confirmation is celebrated or of the candidates, and has some catechetical relationship with the candidates or did the baptism itself.[12] Not only does this affect the traditional episcopal hegemony regarding confirmation in the Roman Rite, but it makes practicable a closer connection between it and the other two sacraments of initiation, baptism and the eucharist, according to the theological principle of (34) mentioned above. This is a large step taken toward restoring a correct initiatory sequence, and it should affect for the better pastoral practice and theological reflection of these three sacraments. Far from constituting a restriction on episcopal ministry, it enhances this ministry by emphasizing the real sacramental importance of the bishop as the one who normally should preside throughout the whole process of Christian initiation. Formerly this ministry was exercised almost wholly in confirmation.

Another structural clarification touches the two anointings with chrism, the one immediately after baptism and the other in confirmation. Since two chrismations so closely conjoined appear cumbersome, the document omits the postbaptismal chrismation when confirmation is to follow directly (224). This clarification of structure is not, however, accompanied with an enlargement of language such a change seems to require. By this I mean that the prayer to be said at the postbaptismal chrismation speaks of the meaning of the act in terms of the neophyte's being anointed "As Christ was anointed Priest, Prophet, and King," so that he or she may always live as a member of his body, the church (224). The prayer said for chrismation at confirmation speaks, instead, of the neophyte's being given the Holy Spirit and his sevenfold gifts (230). Thus, when confirmation is celebrated with baptism the chrismation after baptism is christic and messianic in character. It could be argued that, in this particular case, a structural anomaly has been exchanged for a verbal one.

The confirmation rite concludes with a greeting of the neophyte but, unhappily as it seems, not with the kiss of peace (231). This may be due to the Roman Rite's placing the kiss of peace later, just before communion. Yet one would think that the final act of the whole baptismal synaxis, culminating as it does years of catechesis and many rites preparatory to this moment, is the perfect place for the first exchange of Christian peace between the presiding minister and the neophytes—and perhaps from them extending to the whole congregation. It would be a valid development were the emotional demands of so intense a sacramental moment to give rise to the solemn exchange of peace at this point, just as the first eucharist of Easter day is about to begin.

A fourth and final matter deserves comment since it arises out of the preceding remarks. Unlike the ethos of the old rubrics, which was restrictive on the minister to the point of moral and legal sanctions, the rubrics of this new rite are elastic, expansive, and leave avenues toward further development open in light of future pastoral experience in the use of the rite. In addition, the rite provides a host of options for use by ministers who will certainly find themselves in situations that demand liturgical adaptations to varying cultures and circumstances. This is simply liturgical good sense. The forms given are not "restrictive" but *normative*. As such they presume that local specifications of the general norm both will and must be made. Yet these specific local norms will still be able to recognize one another, for their common parent will be the same—this *Ordo Initiationis Christianae adultorum* of 1972. If episcopal conferences and individual bishops will allow informed and normal liturgical evolution to begin in the manner wisely forseen in the document, and if the celebration of its rites as valid outcomes of a renewed catechumenal discipline is responsibly done in local churches, the result cannot be other than a more catholic Roman initiation polity. And because the church is constantly coming into existence through conversion and sacramental initiation, the result cannot also be other than a more effective and catholic Roman Catholicism. This last result will inevitably be of enormous ecumenical importance for the future.

Period of Postbaptismal Catechesis or Mystagogia (37–40)

It is clear that conversion does not end with the sacraments of initiation. Rather, conversion in Christ among his holy people becomes the public possession of the whole local church each time initiation is brought to term in its premier sacramental phase. Because of this, the Christian community more easily becomes a continuously converting people as it has regular access to the experience of individuals who move through the final stages of initiation each year.

The document makes it equally clear, however, that initiation does not end with baptism, confirmation, and first eucharist at Easter. If the entire initiation sequence from pre-evangelization through first eucharist has been well calibrated, the stunning physical and emotional impact of the sacraments of initiation celebrated in the early hours of Easter morning should throw open a new dimension of the neophyte's consciousness that would permit deeper levels of faith to be articulated—levels that would have been, literally, unspeakable beforehand. If the catechumenal instructions have been more along the lines of a Christian ethic and of how to live a Christian life—instructions typified by a practical concreteness that was at the same time suffused with a realistic and reticent reverence concerning the deeper mysteries of faith—the postbaptismal instructions can be more frankly theological and splendid in their scope.

This distinction between the character of prebaptismal and postbaptismal instruction is not easy to clarify. An illustration of it may, however, be detected by contrasting the ethos of the prebaptismal instruction sketched in the first six chapters of the *Didache* (ca. 100) with that of the postbaptismal homilies of such later fathers as Ambrose of Milan, [13] Cyril of Jerusalem[14] and John Chrysostom.[15] The latter rise to lyric heights in describing the mysteries into which the neophytes had only recently been baptized.[16] Chrysostom, for example, counts the "honors of baptism" in a sermon to the neophytes that fairly shimmers with cosmic symbolism in comparing the baptized to the fire by which the stars burn: "You are not only free, but also holy; not only holy, but also just; not only just, but also sons; not only sons, but also heirs; not only heirs, but also brothers of Christ; not only brothers of Christ, but also joint heirs; not only joint heirs, but also members; not only members, but also the temple; not only the temple, but also instruments of the Spirit. Blessed be God, who alone does wonderful things!"[17]

The rationale underlying postbaptismal catechesis or *mystagogia* should be seen not as having to do with some sort of *disciplina arcani* but with the pedagogical fact that it is next to impossible to discourse effectively about experiences of great moment and intensity with someone who has never really had such an experience. One cannot speak tellingly of love to the unloving. Those who do love, moreover, speak not in analytical or discursive terms but in the language of poetry, music, and symbol. While the period of postbaptismal *mystagogia* is an ancient church structure, its *raison d'être* is as valid as it ever was, given the document's view of conversion climaxing in sacramental initiation. The archaic is not the obsolete.[18]

Thus the document specifies that the main Sunday masses of the Easter season should contain not only homiletic instructions for the neophytes and the whole local church, these masses should also provide that the newly baptized retain their special places in the church (236) and that the readings for these Sundays may always be those contained in the new lectionary for year A.[19] What is expected to happen during this period is that both the community and the neophytes

> ... move forward together meditating on the Gospel, sharing in the eucharist, performing the works of charity. In this way they understand the paschal mystery more fully and bring it into their lives more and more. The period of postbaptismal catechesis or mystagogia is the final period of initiation of the newly baptized (37).

To close the period of postbaptismal catechesis, around Pentecost Sunday, it is suggested that some form of celebration for the neophytes be held. The same is recommended for the anniversary of their baptism. Furthermore, the bishop is urged to "... make sure, especially if he cannot preside at the sacraments of initiation, that at least once a year he meets the newly baptized and presides at a celebration of the eucharist" (239).

Conclusions

If *lex orandi legem statuit credendi* is a valid theological assertion, and if this new order of initiation of adults is to be implemented according to its stated meaning and intent, then all the local churches that make up the Roman communion need to take several matters most seriously.

Clearly, the document is concretely specific on who a Christian is. He is not merely a set of abstract yet imponderable good intentions that are essentially incommunicable and subjectively sovereign. Rather, a Christian is a person of faith in Jesus Christ dead and risen among his faithful people. This faith is no mere noetic thing but a way of living together; it is the bond which establishes that reciprocal mutuality of relationships we call communion, and it is this communion which constitutes the ecclesial real presence of Jesus Christ in the world of grace, faith, hope, charity, and character.

This is what the eucharist celebrates, signifies, and causes within the community of the faithful: it is the church. This is what initiation in the fullest sense disciplines one for: it is the church. All other sacraments and sacramentals—from matrimony to holy orders to penance, anointing of the sick, vows and blessings—find their meaning and purpose only within this "economic" context. All a Christian's rights, privileges, and duties originate here. Here the church's mission is constantly being set at the most fundamental level. Here the obligations to service and the limits on power and authority are established for all ministries within the church, ordained or not. Initiation defines simultaneously both the Christian and the church, and the definition is unsubordinated to any other except the gospel itself, no matter from what source other definitions may originate.

This being the case, I cannot imagine how theological discourse, canonical reform, religious education, ministerial training programs, and even the practical day-to-day running of dioceses and parishes will find it possible not to take as their starting points the present document. For what it contains is not merely some more ceremonial changes for use *ad libitum*. Its core is an ecclesiology of rich existential concreteness and disciplinary clarity arising out of the best that two thousand years of Christian tradition has to offer.

A word about tradition may be in order here, since the profound traditionalism of the document is sure to be interpreted by some as antiquarianism. While I think there are, perhaps, some instances of antiquarianism in the document, use of the provided rites will quickly reveal what these are; then they can be either recast or dropped. But their presence should not blind us to the fact that what is old may also be truly traditional (there is no such thing as a new tradition). Understood correctly, tradition is merely a word denoting those aspects of a group's social compact which have managed to survive the traumas of history *because they work in maintaining the social compact as a whole*. It is by this compact that the group coheres and is thus able to survive. Because of this, the social compact—however it is stated or left unstated—is the result of the entire group and its deliberative processes. The buck stops with the group itself and cannot be appealed to anyone's private "revelation," nor ought it to be taken from the group and handed over to anyone less than the total body politic.[20] In an ecclesial sense, tradition constitutes the summary consensus of the church's total body politic, past as well as present, on points of the most crucial concern to the entire group. Thus differing from mere custom and convention, tradition frees from the tyranny of the present and protects against aggression by the compulsively articulate as well as against opportunism by unchecked authority.

The *Order of Christian Initiation of Adults* represents that aspect of the social compact of the total body politic of the church on the matter of who a Christian is and what, therefore, communities of Christians ought to be. As such, the document amounts to a sort of constitutional bill of rights for the whole of the church's membership that is meant to be not only read and understood but enacted regularly in sacramental modes that are efficacious of their content. *Sacramenta significando efficiunt gratiam.*[21]

If one factors into this theological focal point the main alterations in initiatory polity contained in the document, it becomes obvious how truly radical a renewal of church life may result. The main alterations I perceive in the document are these: First, the initiation of adults is regarded as the normal practice. Second, a catechumenate of serious content and duration is made again a standard church structure. Third, the ministry of confirmation is opened up to presbyters in a good many circumstances. Fourth, the reason for the foregoing is to secure a closer proximity of confirmation to baptism within the same liturgical event. Fifth, the document insists that there is, in addition, a most ·serious theological and sacramental set of reasons for this closer connection: it ". . . signifies the unity of the paschal mystery, the close relationship between the mission of the Son and the pouring out of the Holy Spirit, and the joint celebration of the sacraments by which the Son and the Spirit come with the Father upon those who are baptized" (34). Sixth, the immediately postbaptismal chrismation is omitted when confirmation is to follow, a reform that cannot help but enhance the pneumatic element in sacramental initiation. And seventh, prebaptismal and postbaptismal modes of catechesis are clearly discriminated.

History will judge how adequate we will be in restoring initiatory discipline as conceived of in this document. Rites remain just words on a page until they become an enacted way of life in common. From the admittedly poor vantage point of the present, however, I would hazard that this document may well appear to a writer a century from now as the most important result of the Second Vatican Council for the life of the church. I hazard this, not because of the document's ceremonial details but because of the concrete, robust, and disciplined vision it projects of the church as a community of faith lived in common—a vision it means to be efficaciously enacted over and over again, each year at the center of the church's being as it corporately passes, in Jesus Christ, from death to life by the Spirit. The document's purpose is to reenforce where possible, and recreate where necessary, insights and structures that will reintegrate facets of that life which have been allowed to drift away from each other for a variety of reasons.[22] Rejoining these facets once more into an economy of unique and practical richness in which the divine initiative and faithful human response can meet, interact, and be sustained to a degree not attainable for centuries would alone make this document a major event of promise in the lives of all churches and all Christians everywhere.

NOTES

1. See my "The Norm of Baptism: The New Rite of Christian Initiation of Adults," *Worship* 48 (1974): 143–152.

2. Vatican City: Typis Polyglottis Vaticanis 1972. Since the English translation by the International Committee on English in the Liturgy is imminent, paragraphs to which I shall refer in brackets follow the provisional ICEL text.

3. Kavanagh, "The Norm of Baptism," esp. pp. 146–147.

4. An adequate bibliography on initiation would be too large to include here, but a few works deserve mention. For bibliography and general background see Alois Stenzel, *Die Taufe: eine genetische Erklärung der Taufliturgie* (Innsbruck: F. Rauch, 1958), and B. Neunheuser, *Baptism and Confirmation*, trans. J. J. Hughes (New York: Herder and Herder, 1964). E. C. Whitaker, *Documents of the Baptismal Liturgy* (London: S.P.C.K., 1960); L. L. Mitchell, *Baptismal Anointing*, Alcuin Club Collections 48 (London: S.P.C.K., 1966); J. D. C. Fisher, *Christian Initiation: Baptism in the Medieval West*, Alcuin Club Collections 47 (London: S.P.C.K., 1965) and *Christian Initiation: The Reformation Period*, Alcuin Club Collections 51 (London:

S.P.C.K., 1970); P. J. Jagger, *Christian Initiation 1552–1969*, Alcuin Club Collections 52 (London: S.P.C.K., 1970).

5. Emphasis added for *Ecclesia, munere suo apostolico jungens.* The point is of theological moment since admission to the catechumenate is characterized as an act of the church's apostolic function. This seems rather much if admission to the catechumenate is merely a preliminary formality of little or no ecclesiological or sacramental importance. The wording of (14) suggests contrary: that the "membership" spoken of as being the result of this apostolic act on the church's part is not the result of baptism but of being a catechumen. Such membership is ecclesial because it aggregates one into a whole set of personal and structural relationships that are public and sacramental in nature, i.e., the whole catechumenal structure that follows.

6. Kavanagh, "The Norm of Baptism," p. 147.

7. For precedents see J. A. Jungmann, *The Mass of the Roman Rite I*, trans. F. A. Brunner (New York: Benziger, 1951): 474–480.

8. See B. Fischer, "Baptismal Exorcism in the Catholic Baptismal Rites after Vatican II," *Studia Liturgica* 10 (1974): 48–55.

9. See the vigil readings from the Hebrew Bible: Gen. 1:1–2:2 (creation), Gen. 22:1–18 (Abraham's sacrifice of Isaac), Exod. 14:15–15:1 (the passage through the Red Sea), Isa. 54:5–14 (God's mercy for Israel), Isa. 55:1–11 (God's covenant), Bar 3:9–15, 34 and 4:4 (the fountain of wisdom), Ezek. 36:16–28 (pure water and a new heart).

10. R. W. Emerson, "An Address delivered before the Senior Class in Divinity College, Cambridge, Sunday Evening, July 15, 1838," *The Prose Works of Ralph Waldo Emerson* I (Boston: Fields, Osgood, 1870): 977.

11. Hippolytus suggests as much, saying: "And so each one drying himself, they shall put on their clothes, and after this let them be together in the assembly." Immediately there follows a description of the bishop's imposition of hands and anointing of the neophytes, after which he imparts to them for the first time the kiss of peace. *Ap. Trad.* 21.19–22.6. Cf. G. Dix (ed.), *The Treatise on the Apostolic Tradition of St. Hippolytus of Rome*, 2nd ed. (London: S.P.C.K., 1968): 38–39. On what Episcopalians are doing on this matter, see L. Mitchell, "Revision of the Rites of Christian Initiation in the American Episcopal Church," *Studia Liturgica* 10 (1974): 25–34.

12. "When the bishop is absent, the presbyter who baptizes an adult or a child of catechetical age should also confer confirmation, unless this sacrament is to be given at another time (e.g., during the postbaptismal catechesis period or on Pentecost "in certain cases" (56)). When there are very many to be confirmed, the minister of the sacrament of confirmation may associate other presbyters with himself in its administration" (46; see also 228).

13. Ambroise de Milan, *Des Sacrements. Des Mystères. Explication du Symbole*, ed. by B. Botte, Sources Chrétiennes 25 (Paris: Editions du Cerf, 1961). For English cf. *St. Ambrose, On the Sacraments and On the Mysteries*, ed. J. H. Srawley, trans. T. Thompson (London: S.P.C.K., 1950).

14. *Cyrille du Jerusalem, Catécheses Mystagogiques*, ed A. Piédagnel, Sources Chrétiennes 126 (Paris: Editions du Cerf, 1966). For English see *St. Cyril of Jerusalem's Lectures on the Christian Sacraments*, ed. F. L. Cross, (London: S.P.C.K., 1951).

15. *St. Jean Chrysostome, Huit catécheses baptismales inédites*, ed. A. Wenger, Sources Chrétiennes 50 (Paris: Editions du Cerf, 1957). For English

St. John Chrysostom, Baptismal Instructions, trans./ed. P. W. Harkins, Ancient Christian Writers 31 (Westminster, Maryland: Newman Press, 1963).

16. For an effective recreation of the patristic setting of the *mystagogia,* see F. van der Meer, *Augustine the Bishop,* trans. B. Battershaw and G. R. Lamb (New York: Sheed & Ward, 1961): 347–387; 453–467.

17. Cited in *Baptism: Ancient Liturgies and Patristic Texts,* ed. A. Hamman (Staten Island: Alba House, 1967): 166. Compare this with Chrysotom's homily to the elect at the beginning of Lent in the same volume pp. 139–151. A close comparison of even this one father's prebaptismal and postbaptismal homilies could benefit those who would establish catechumenates according to the letter and spirit of the new order of adult baptism.

18. See V. Turner, "Passages, Margins, and Poverty: Religious Symbols of Communitas," *Worship* 46 (1972): 390–412 and 482–494, esp. 391.

19. These texts may also be used for the mystagogical period even when sacramental initiation is consummated at some other time of the year (40).

20. Paul Ramsey raises the same issue, in a civil context, concerning the judiciary's "privatizing" the decision on who is to be regarded as human and thus possessing a valid claim to rights in our society: "Protecting the Unborn," *Commonweal* 100 (31 May 1974): 308–314. The same issue also may be detected in the current process of presidential impeachment.

21. K. Rahner, *The Church and the Sacraments,* trans. W. J. O'Hara (New York: Herder and Herder, 1963): 34–40. Cf. Council of Trent, session VII, canon 6, *Enchiridion Symbolorum,* 33rd ed., ed. by Denzinger-Schönmetzer (Freiburg: Herder, 1965): num. 1606.

22. See J. D. C. Fisher, *Christian Initiation: Baptism in the Medieval West* for a description of this disintegration in initiatory structures. Also the useful summary article of G. Wainwright, "The Rites and Ceremonies of Christian Initiation," *Studia Liturgica* 10 (1974):2–24.

CHAPTER VII

Christian Initiation:
The State of the Question

Ralph A. Keifer

IT IS IRONIC THAT WE HAVE SO OFTEN CRIED OUT TO ROME TO TURN RADI-
cal, so often expecting in turn obscurantism, time serving, and
conservatism of a conventional sort, that we have not been able to
perceive radical revision and drastic change when Rome presents
us with it. As far as the liturgical books are concerned, that is
precisely the change Rome has undertaken, reversing a thousand
years of practices and attitudes. This change has gone unnoticed,
virtually without comment, and with scarcely a word of dissent.
Under the aegis of an ecumenical council, with the approval of the
Roman see, and over the signature of the Roman pontiff, the
primary rites of initiation (those for the baptism and confirmation
of adults and the baptism of children) have been turned upside
down and inside out, heralding a cry to begin a reform and
renewal of the most radical sort.

What has Rome done? First of all, it has restored the baptismal
focus of the paschal season from Lent through Pentecost, design-
ing a lectionary and a sacramentary which are only fully intelligible when the paschal celebration revolves around the baptizing
of adults whose catechumenate has been brought to a head during
Lent, and whose initiation is the central event of the liturgical
year. This practice is, moreover, designed not only for "mission
countries" but for the universal church. The new rite for the
initiation of adults is but the elaboration of this central refocusing,
just as the new rite for the baptism of children presumes a local
church which has come to grips with the full meaning of baptism
as elaborated according to lectionary, sacramentary, and adult rite.

Second, such a revision represents a radical change of sacramental symbols and priorities. Instead of being an occasional hurried service for infants, and an exceptional one for a few adults, but nonetheless equally hurried and as private as possible, Christian initiation has become not merely a public event in the church, but *the* public event. For the celebration of the paschal mystery finds its axis and its concrete manifestation in the baptism, confirmation, and eucharist of newly baptized adults, prepared for by the whole church during all of Lent, exulted over during the pentecostal fifty days after Easter, and re-evoked by the weekly Sunday eucharist. The revelation of Christ's saving, healing, and redeeming power in our midst is the making of Christians. That all people should now become primordial sacramental signs is a breathtaking departure from the recent past.

Third, such drastic revision and innovation represents a departure in pastoral priorities and perspectives, a departure so radical that it has been unparalleled since the middle ages and well before. The new initiatory perspective rejects the pastoral assumption that an implicit faith, appropriated in and through a Christian culture, is an acceptable standard for lay life. The norm of pastoral care becomes, not the preservation of a faith already assumed to be present and nurtured mainly outside of the formal structure of the liturgy, but the radical transformation of life and values, publicly celebrated as a corporate responsibility.

Fourth, the new perspective signals the end of the divorce between liturgy and life, between private devotion and public function, between active ministers and inert laity. It assumes that the liturgy will be a manifestation of the real life lived by the church, a life marked by sufficient conversion to be worth celebrating, sufficient conversion and catechesis to perceive that the proclamation of the wonderful works of God is possible because they occur among us, sufficient conversion to ensure that the laity are not the passive recipients of hierarchical grace but that ministry made sacramental in orders is a mirror of the priestly service of the entire people of God. The real nature of Christian ministry as collegial, shared, and mutual is revealed in the preparation of catechumens. The candidates for baptism are not only the recipients of the church's ministry, they are ministers to the church as well. For it is their experience of transformation which witnesses the presence and power of the risen Lord to the church.

There is an exception, and if I am to address myself properly to the topic at hand, I cannot fail to note it. At first sight, the consistency applied to sacramentary, lectionary, and rites of adult and child baptism was not carried through with regard to confirmation. The medieval decomposition of Christian initiation into an occasional and minimal private service, the ossification of the lenten and paschal liturgies, and the divorce between paschal celebration and initiation, were all developments which the present reform rejects root and branch. Yet the medieval development of confirmation as something separate from baptism has been retained. It must be observed, however, that this separation is not presented as a normative pattern, for adults are to be confirmed immediately after baptism. The exception for children, however, is liable to give us trouble. The sacramental unity, manifest in a catechumenate which takes place during Lent and which culminates in the paschal vigil where the threefold initiatory rite takes place, is not a unity which is served by letting the confirmation of children dangle loose apart from baptism and eucharist.

Of course there is the widespread and novel notion that confirmation is a sacrament of commitment and maturity. Such a view tends to do violence to the biblical and patristic traditions on the question of baptism, for it makes of baptism a kind of catechumenal preparation for life in the church. If baptism is as irrevocable as we claim it to be, and if it is in fact, as bible and liturgy affirm it to be, a passage from death to the life of the risen Lord and of his spirit (and note that these two are radically inseparable correlatives), then we cannot baptize and hope that some of those who are baptized will one day become real Christians. At the same time, it must be observed that many who support the maturity-commitment view of confirmation are seriously concerned with a number of values reflected in the rest of the initiatory continuum: a priority is given to the experience of transformation which is initiation; a priority is given to responsible acceptance of the gospel; a priority is given to making the experience of conversion and transformation visible and public before the whole church. But if these priorities are to be valued over and above the desirability of incorporating children of Christian families into the full sacramental life of the church, and prior to the witness to the sovereignty of God's grace which infant baptism is, then we must abandon infant baptism, not exalt confirmation. And if we are to retain infant baptism, it seems only sensible that it must be followed by infant confirmation and communion.

The problem with retaining the practice of confirmation at a later age and interpreting it as a sacrament of commitment or maturity is that it does serious damage to the understanding of a sacrament as an action of God as well as an action of man. Man's commitment is not the measure of God's grace. Moreover, there is no such thing as a fully "mature" Christian this side of the *eschaton*. Perhaps we should consider the approach proposed by the Episcopal Church in this country, which unifies initiation while providing for a repeatable rite as the reaffirmation of the baptismal commitment. Alternatively, we might consider the enrollment of children as catechumens and the deferral of full initiation to a later age. At any rate, the present practice is a theological and pastoral anomaly. It separates the gift of the Spirit from entry into the body of the risen Lord, violates a sacramental continuum, and leads to a notion that there are degrees of membership in the church among the baptized.

The problems of the appropriate age and place of confirmation, however, are only minor compared to the pastoral problem of translating the norms of the liturgical books into concrete practice. The clear intent of the reform is that initiation should be experiential, not only for those who are initiated, but also, and equally important, for the local church which does the initiating.

Here is the pastoral difficulty. The conception of church as local communion in faith, as vehicle of the experience of the risen Lord, as eschatological sign, exists only in official text and clerical rhetoric, not as something perceived by the great majority of churchgoers. Our operative model is still that of the established church, a bastion of conservation, convention, and respectability. For most of us the Church is not a dynamic and communal reality, but a static institution which ministers to the needs of individuals who occasionally present themselves. For many, the church is not a "we" but a "they" or an "it." The standard by which church life is measured is not conversion but conformity, and a minimal one at that. That conversion should be a matter of any kind of experience, much less of corporate experience, is not expected and not really desired. If anyone publically rises above the minimal conformity, the community suspects that what is in its hands is either an incipient fanatic or an incipient religious vocation. As a result, the pieties and strongly evocative symbols of the preconciliar church have virtually disappeared—and with them the sense of being a people. We are in a real sense less a community of faith now than we were a decade ago. An extremely brittle authority structure and narrow symbolic focus have cracked, and with them a sense of distinctiveness and belonging which characterized preconciliar Catholicism. As a result, to speak of initiation is extremely problematic because there is so little to initiate people *into,* and little or nothing to celebrate. It should not be surprising that so many attempts at liturgy are lackluster, banal, conventional and boring. Boredom is, after all, the experience of having to attend constantly to the insignificant.

Another factor in the present situation is the confusion of catechesis with education and the simultaneous confusion of education with the dissemination of information. All too often it is forgotten that education must rest on an adequate social base. It is impossible to educate people to the values of a nonexistent group. Thus, the phenomenon of the past ten years has been to use a new rhetoric without changing much of the reality which is the local church. Our present catechetics continually put us in the position of telling people, "Yes, Virginia, there is a church." The church, however, is not the focus of a strong corporate identity. Rather, it is a temporary and part-time associational structure which, like other such structures in our lives, compels something less than avid enthusiasm and something less than full commitment. The church to many minds is a spiritual feeding station, not an eschatological community of the Spirit.

And it is also a church which can only be described as schizophrenic. Why is such a description apt? All one need do is walk into any ordinary parish church, at any time. We have cast our situation in our own ikons. In the background, the old marble altar with its candles and decorations stands flanked by the American and papal flags. In the foreground, a rickety wooden table stands littered with leaflets and papers. There we are as a church. On one hand, we still live with an inappropriate past, utterly immovable, cluttering the way, and exerting its inexorable influence. On the other hand, we loudly proclaim that we are as

American as anybody else. But we are American not as black music is American, not as Shaker furniture is American, not as the New England meetinghouse is American. We are American not as Faulkner or Willa Cather, but American as the pollution of Lake Erie, as beaches littered with flip tops, as houses not forty years old and in shambles, as health care that sucks away the lifeblood of the destitute. We are as American as the quick solution, the throwaway art, the despising of all that is not obvious, instantly perceptible, and of immediate pragmatic relevance. We are as American as the tolerance of all ugliness except human misery, which can be hidden away in nursing homes and ghettos and buried under rhetoric.

As well as being American almost to the point of obscenity, we have retained the pastoral patterns of an established church which has a European heritage. Within that situation, the assumption was that church and culture were, or ought to be, virtually coterminous. Baptism of infants *quamprimum* became the initiatory norm for people who were to become Christian by cultural osmosis. The overriding consideration was the removal of original sin from the child. If there were questions about the capacity of the parents to form the child in faith, these were at best secondary questions, and in a pinch the child was to be given the benefit of the doubt. It was assumed that a Catholic culture—either the milieu of the Catholic countries of Western Europe, or later, an American sub-culture fostered by the parochial school and a host of parish organizations—would be the locus for the Christian formation of the child.

There was no expectation that initiation would be any sort of experiential and concrete transformation and theologians, hard pressed to make sense of biblical and patristic data on initiation, were forced to stand on their heads to talk about the *infusion* of this, that, and the other into passive infants. Still less was there any concern that such transformation should be a corporate event witnessed and celebrated by the whole church. Baptism took place quietly in a corner, even more quietly in a corner for the rare adult, so as not to cause embarrassment by the perceived incongruity of submitting people to something which ought to have been done in infancy. To be sure, shreds and relics of the old initiatory focus lay buried in the Lenten and paschal liturgies; but in their mummified form, only a scholar could recognize them. Popular piety ignored them altogether, as did rubrical and canonical norms which prevented their pastoral utilization. Conversion, the experience of transformation in Christ, was ritualized in a living way only in religious orders, with a theology of second baptism attached to vows. To a certain extent, it was also realized in the gradual transmutation of the presbyterate into a mystique of the priest as *alter Christus*. Behind this approach was a radical shift of the church's missionary focus, a shift which began with the cessation of persecution in the fourth century, and which was clearly evident by the time of the conversion of Clovis in the eighth century.

Up to the fourth century, and in part well beyond it, the primary focus of the church's mission was the appropriation of the Gospel by individual persons, not isolated individuals but individuals called to live in a community of faith and in the world. That this approach condemned the church to a quasi-monastic or sectarian existence was due, more than anything else, to the consciously pagan character of public life in the ancient world. Again and again it was the problem of idolatry as a fact of virtually all spheres of public life which forced the church to remain a separate enclave within the culture of the ancient world. It is clear, both from the refusal to compromise with the idolatrous state and the immense concern for such things as concrete care for the poor, that the church's evangelization of individuals had nothing in common with modern approaches to a gospel of personal salvation which elicits no concern for justice, and which gladly joins in contemporary versions of emperor worship. As long as the church's primary emphasis was a mission to persons, the liturgy of initiation retained its vigor. For it was through the corporate experience of conversion that the church sustained its identity in the world. The church did not look to the culture for support or sustenance, much less for formation.

With the conversion of Constantine, on the other hand, the church began to look to the christianization of culture: its concern, so to speak, became the baptism of institutions, a concern to baptize from the top of society downward. The approach is effectually signified by the numerous ecclesiastical emissaries, usually bishops, sent to the courts of kings. Such an approach is a far cry from St. Paul rejoicing because he can proclaim the gospel to the imperial guard and a far cry from the anonymous spread of the gospel by simple faithful which characterized the church in its earliest period.

The focus on institutions rather than persons resulted in a dependence upon culture to sustain Christian life and Christian identity. It also resulted in an objectification of Christian symbols of transformation and a transposition of conversion from an experiential to a vicarious reality. All of these converged in a radical change of eschatology. As the sense of individual conversion and corporate celebration of that conversion diminished, the coming of the kingdom bifurcated into something seen either as wholly future and individualistic or as realized in institutions. The majority of the laity, who now experienced themselves as "poor banished children of Eve, exiles in this valley of tears," pinned their hopes on surrogates (clergy and religious), on vicarious symbols of transformation (saints and holy objects), and on a wholly future conversion (getting out of purgatory). On the other hand, church institutions were a manifestation of realized eschatology, forever fixed, immutable, perfect, and ideal ("individuals are sinners but the church is holy"). In between, the sense of the local concrete church as the body of Christ, locale of the Spirit, sign of the coming kingdom, receded to be replaced by a sacral few, ministering to an indifferent many.

The tacit assumption of this system was that the only thing expected of the laity was conventional religiosity, which was manifest in a compliance with certain minimal regulations. There was little expectation that they would have any capacity to undergo lasting transformation, a conviction signaled in legislation which assumed as a matter of course that all of the laity would fall into mortal sin during the course of a year—hence the requirement for yearly confession.

It is not surprising that the western church found itself incapable of articulating a theology of the Spirit. In the dichotomy between church as sacral institution and individual as minimal Christian, the Spirit became simply the legitimator of static institutions or an occasional *deus ex machina* to bail out individuals in time of trouble. In such a bifurcated situation, it was impossible to develop the sense of church as a communion in the Spirit, where ministry is not merely vertical, i.e., from sacred ministers to ordinary laity, but also horizontal, i.e., from one to another without discrimination of office. It is often noted that a strong pneumatology was frequently characteristic of sectarian protest. And rightly so, because it was only in such circles that the identification between church and culture was rejected.

This heritage of the established church is not at all irrelevant to the present status of Christian initiation. The fundamental assumptions of the system survived the Reformation virtually intact. The result of the Tridentine reform was ultimately to raise the tone of Catholic life, but it was a reform along conservative lines. The ineffectualness of the model in the modern world has only been slowly acknowledged by the church, and it has only become apparent as urbanization and political, scientific, and industrial revolution have meant an increasing alienation of most Europeans from the life of the church. In this country, where the church was by law not established, it still retained most of the features of the established church. A vigorous attempt to maintain a Catholic subculture was pursued, especially through schools and parochial and diocesan organizations. At the same time, however, there was an equally vigorous attempt to be as American as possible. The result was that American Catholic identity was generally bound up with ethnicity, distinctive devotional practices, a divergence from others on one or two points of bedroom morality, and precious little else. There was virtually no attempt to evangelize those who were not ethnically Catholic, and virtually no attempt to criticize most American values—sure signs that the pattern of the established church was still operative. American Catholicism saw itself as an agent of conservation, not of transformation.

Now that the waves of immigration are essentially two generations behind us, the aftermath of World War II has steadily eroded the ethnic neighborhood, and devotional life has been affected both by assimilation to the presuppositions of a Protestant culture and by a liturgical reform which disturbed the symbiosis between private devotion and ancient rite, even these slender ties of Catholic identity have been loosened. Since the presupposition of the established church is that religious identity and meaning will largely be forged by a culture which is conceived to be fundamentally Christian, we are in for serious trouble. In the modern world, where the Christian direction of culture is at best highly ambiguous, the retention of a pattern appropriate to the established church implies the retention of pastoral patterns which presume rather than attempt to evoke its radical conversion; an undirected and uncritical assimilation of the values of the culture as a whole; and the retention of ecclesiastical institutions in an ossified and progressively more ineffective form, accompanied by a progressive erosion of those institutions as the values of the culture are assimilated and work against them.

The first is evident in the present inability of the church to say no to any who present themselves for sacramental incorporation into the church. It is not surprising that it cannot say no. It does not even know what questions it should put to those who so present themselves. It does not dare to ask whether they can pray, whether they live as disciples and servants of other members of the local church, whether they know how to make their occupations and professions a ministry for justice in the world, or whether they can give a real account of the hope that is in them. The church does not even dare ask such questions of those who approach the Lord's table on a Sunday morning, because its worship operates in the fashion of the established church with an independent cult, not as expression of ecclesial life. And it does not dare ask such questions because it does not have the means to provide concrete answers.

Regarding the second point, since the church tends to operate as an establishment, it speaks mainly through its officers and at a distance. As a result, it can only exhort. It has no means to be a reflective body with regard to issues of import outside the church door. Moreover—and this is the other side of the coin of assuming conversion—it is unable to challenge, because it knows that in reality it demands only minimal commitment. To demand, all of a sudden, more than this, is to ask more than the market will bear. Those who criticize bishops for not taking strong stands on a variety of issues are less in touch with the church than the bishops themselves who know how unprepared we are for challenge.

As regards the third point, since the church has no firm sense of identity with its past, and no clear vision of a future which does not include establishment, it is forced to stand between arcane conservatism and cheap relevance. This is the reason why we

Christians end up being such bundles of contradiction. We are religiously schizophrenic because we tend to rock between assumptions resting on an irrelevant, outmoded, mostly inoperative ecclesial model on the one hand, and on the other, assumptions resting on an uncritical appropriation of less than Christian values of our culture. The result is a church incapable of initiating, because it is incapable of living and acting as a community of faith into which people can be initiated. As we stand at present, people can be partially assimilated but they cannot be initiated. The reason is that we function as an aggregate, not as a community. Moreover, all of our initiatory symbols are symbols of transformation, and if there is anything the present church does not stand for it is transformation. It merely oscillates between conservation and capitulation. This is one of the reasons why it is such a common occurrence to find individual clergy who attempt to combine a conception of themselves as both shaman and social worker, and also why it is not difficult to find people who simultaneously maintain that religion is merely man's search for ultimate meaning and that they accept papal infallibility, or to find people who are untroubled by intercommunion but believe that Protestants are crypto-atheists, or who freely substitute the writings of unbelievers for the scriptures but never fail to recite the eucharistic *verba*, or who insist upon daily concelebration of the eucharist while despising the divine office.

The reasons for our schizophrenia are cultural and historical, since we have blended the heritage of the established church with the American melting pot. Against this cultural drift, the new initiatory rites are, for all practical purposes, impotent, because those who use them are the products and shapers of that very same culture. If we continue to accept this cultural drift, we will use the new initiatory rites, just as we have used everything else in the Roman books, grudgingly, and with no attempt to form a community of faith which might be fit to celebrate them. Instead, we will continue with the vain hope that education will do the job. In the meantime, theologians will continue to go hunting under the cultural bed for appropriate American symbols, while the church will continue the process of cultural adaptation, and our funeral parlor piety will assure that wine, water, embraces, real people, and the like never really surface as viable symbols. Celebrants will retain their fundamental notion of liturgy as independent cult, spending far more time at drama workshops and committee meetings than they do in prayer or in the gutsy interaction called catechesis. As regards the norms set forth in the liturgical books, excepting the most obvious rubrics, they can be ignored as unintelligible, unwanted, and unenforceable. And so we may stumble on, pasting American civil religion with its sentimentality, its pelagianism, and its massive pride, on rites neither understood nor appreciated.

It can be conceded that there are a variety of hopeful exceptions to the drift just described, but they are exceptions. They are hopeful in the sense that they present less an actuality than a remote possibility that we might come to grips with the cultural situation which we now face. There are not many strong indications that the American church as a whole is presently prepared to accept the implications of the new rites of initiation.

The only group of any size which comes even close to appropriating the kind of baptismal piety required by the new rites of initiation is the Catholic pentecostal movement. Yet it remains wedded to an impoverished evangelical protestant mode of articulation, to say nothing of a world-view which is insufficiently incarnational for it to be taken seriously by the wider church. At the same time, some of its central assertions cannot be taken lightly. The pentecostal insistence that the paschal mystery is first of all an event and an experience, and only secondly a doctrine is precisely the assertion of our new initiatory rites. Moreover, there are more ways than one in which the question of the transforming power of the Spirit is relevant to the issue of initiation.

The attempt to reform the rites of initiation has issued in the promulgation of rites which are, historically and cuturally speaking, a massive rejection of the presuppositions both of pastoral practice and of most churchgoers regarding the true meaning of Church membership. This is a revolution quite without precedent, because the Catholic Church has never at any time in its history done such violence to its ritual practice as to make its rites so wholly incongruous with its concrete reality. Such an act is either a statement that rite is wholly irrelevant, or a statement that the church is willing to change, and to change radically, that concrete reality. Such an approach is either suicide or prophecy of a very high order. The past use of ancient and mysterious rituals which made few demands on the individual and virtually none on the congregation was perfectly congruous and relevant to the symbiosis between established church and modern culture. This point was made brutally clear by the baptismal scene in *The Godfather*. The new rites, with their enormous demand on the individual and on the local church, are neither congruous with nor relevant to the popular presuppositions as to what the church is all about. As it has already done with regard to the eucharist, the implementation of new rites may accelerate decay and attrition by loosening one more tie with the past. An act of God will be required to make it possible for our people to accept such a radical change. This is not to suggest that we sit around and do nothing, but only to point out that the pastoral problem of bringing the local church to a real, vivid, engaging celebration of initiation as the focus of the church's life and reality is far more immense than we may imagine.

We have a massive religious problem on our hands because the paschal mystery is, to most people, a near-abstraction. The dying and rising of Christ is perceived more as a past event than as a present reality. If we are going to do any real initiating, we are going to have to become confortable with God-talk, gospel-talk, Jesus-talk, and Spirit-talk which is both convinced and convincing. The community into which we are baptized is not fundamentally an institution but an event, and the event is founded on the personal action of the triune God. We are baptized not simply into a human community, but into the risen Christ and the indwelling Spirit. We are, most of us, horribly inept at communicating this, horribly embarrassed by it, so much so that the homiletic and catechetical Christ is usually presented as an absent lawgiver and teacher and example. God-talk is not the only thing needed for viable evangelization and catechesis, but it is of the utmost priority. Unless we can learn to speak of God as a living and present reality, we are doomed (and the word is appropriate) to failure. There is at present no greater pastoral vacuum than the inability to show people the presence of God in their lives. It is noteworthy that for all the endless talk about ministry of the word, very little of it is directed to the question of the way in which people might be brought to a living awareness that the kingdom of God is indeed among them. For all the discussion of the possibilities of ministry in the church today, what is truly remarkable is the low priority given to any attempt to form ministers who might be willing to take the kind of risk required to articulate for others one's own experience and understanding of a personal God. For all the hand wringing over the inability of people to enter into a spirit of celebration, it is fascinating how little attention has been given to the question of evoking a sense of wonder at the *mirabilia Dei* in the lives of ordinary people. One of the great tragedies of our time is that our notion of ministry is so vertical and so clericalized that we never even ask the question as to what role the sick, the poor, and the suffering might have in ministering to the needs of those who are "whole," especially in meeting the problem of a faith ever more rarefied and removed from reality.

There is also the desperate problem of parochial size, and with it the equally desperate assumption that all ministry must be presbyteral. Little attempt has been made for parishes to break down into smaller units, and even less to suggest that such structuring need not always and everywhere require the services of a priest. Unless we begin to come to grips with this question, our initiatory rites will continue to have the flavor of the incongruous and the peculiar. It is indeed an incongruity to welcome people into a "community" of strangers.

It may seem that my comments are unduly pessimistic. I do not mean to say that nothing is happening in the Church. Rather, I do wish to sound cautious about our new initiatory rites. They are in many ways out of step with the presuppositions of those who must use them. They also provide a possible critique of church life as it is presently lived. For those reasons they are not apt to be received with open arms and they will not be easily understood. Their use is going to prove to be something of a mixed blessing. We risk the danger of making the new rites of initiation wholly unintelligible if we do not raise serious questions about the character of church life. We catholics are all too prone to seek ritual answers to deeper questions. My concern is that we not act as if initiatory problems were solved merely by using new initiatory rites.

CHAPTER VIII

Hope for the Future: A Summary

Robert W. Hovda

THE HISTORY OF CHRISTIAN INITIATION IS, AS ROBERT GRANT HAS pointed out, one of "multiple choices in manifold situations" rather than straight-line development, progress, evolution. "What one sees is not progress but change, brought about as the church responded to various kinds of occasions."[1]

But now that we have grown wise enough to want to live with the Spirit in the present, our past has been opened up to us by tools, by scholarship, by the discovery of sources undreamed of yesterday. True reform, renewal, and reconciliation are thus far more attainable today than they were in the sixteenth or any other century.

Many of us have come a long way in the last few years. In Aidan Kavanagh's terms, we are beginning to ask strategic rather than merely tactical questions. We are coming at our problems from many different avenues and movements, but all are signs of life dedication, rich promises of energy that a more coherent ecclesial life can tap and help to flourish.

These various avenues and movements may seem to be parallel and without juncture, because the local church exists today in a generally unhealthy condition. However, as the local church revives I think we will see a great convergence. We have a liturgical movement, we have a pentecostal and small group prayer movement, we have social and political action movements, we have a catechists' movement, we have a peace movement, we have all kinds of movements of liberation. We have persons and groups of persons putting their bodies, resources, talents, and time into liturgy planning, catechetical programs, works of social ministry, prayer meetings, protest and witness activities. Every one of these avenues or strands is a hook on which we can hang our hopes; every fragment is an invitation to put a way of life together. That way of life is the local church, and its genesis and formation is the process of Christian initiation. Both Robert Grant and Nathan Mitchell have shown how the triumph of infant baptism led to the disintegration and dissolution of that process. Both seem to agree that the process has to be revived in some manner if the local church is to gain any degree of health. In all of the essays in this volume there seems to me to be a consensus or agreement that is most impressive.

In stark contrast to our common practice, we seem to agree that the sacraments of initiation—baptism, confirmation, and eucharist—belong together, most appropriately in the Easter Vigil, whatever the age of the candidates. We seem also to agree that, in the case of the normative adult rite, these sacraments climax a lengthy initiatory process that involves the entire local church and that is experiential as well as instructional.

There seems to be consensus today that a case can be made for the incorporation of infants and children into the church by the same sacraments of initiation. Even though adult initiation remains the norm, that of infants and children is much more common and requires the provision of structures that will foster "initiatory" experiences appropriate to the age and circumstances of the growing and maturing Christian.

We also seem to agree that the initiation process is primarily experiential and only secondarily instructional: a community process, a dialogue, a sharing of prayer, discipline, mission, celebration as well as beliefs, an experience of mutual support and encouragement. With infant baptism the common practice, the clear implication is that the local church must assign an urgent priority to the problem of assuring all its members an opportunity to share in this experience involved in the renewal and reinitiation process connected with baptism every Lent and Easter. In addition to putting the sacraments of initiation back together after their long separation, this seems to me to be the most practical pastoral imperative to emerge from our discussions.

We are talking about initiation into the church, so the church is the key issue. What one does about initiation will depend on one's theology of the church, one's vision of the church. I would like to summarize some ecclesiological issues which will, I think, both indicate the ground we have covered and offer some reason for hope.

A Church That Is Concrete

As long as we thought of the church chiefly in abstract and universal terms (it was always "the church," in the singular), we could skirt these problems and *assume* the Christian foundations of faith, conversion, initiation, community. But reform and renewal are not accomplished in the abstract. Recent years have focused our attention on the local level, on our concrete faith communities and the people who make them up. Now we must begin to realize the full dimensions of those fundamental problems.

Without any diminution of the catholic value and priority of communion among the churches, our attention has been drawn to the local church. For that, as Aidan Kavanagh has said, is the ecclesial structure in which "conversion therapy" is carried on.

> For when we talk about confirmation our conversation is really about baptism; when we are dealing with baptism we are discoursing about Christian Initiation; when we are into initiation we are face to face with conversion in Jesus Christ dead and rising; and when we are into conversion in Jesus Christ dead and rising we are at the storm center of the universe.[2]

Such a "storm center" involves personal crisis or, more likely, repeated personal crises through life. No one can affirm the one true God without rejecting all kinds of pretenders, now as ever. This can be a lonely business, and one cannot survive it all by oneself. Catechesis is the process in which the whole local church community joins hands with the candidates in gestures of mutual support. Lent and Easter annually invite the whole community every year (catechumens or not) to experience the same kind of common strength for starting anew and "getting it all together" again.

When catechesis is postulated as the learning of a set of beliefs or the intellectual grasp of a new concept of life, it conceivably can take place in one's study, by mail, with a book agent. When, however, catechesis is understood as initiation into the lifestyle of a local community of faith, then more is required. Nathan Mitchell has pointed out the importance of the tactile dimension in all sacramental gestures.[3] This tactile dimension is also critical for establishing the concreteness and sacramentality of the local church community. The laying on of hands, for example, seems to be a basic gesture in all sacramental action. Whether it is done in connection with admission into the community or with ministry to the sick, it signifies at the very least the presence of the believing community and its love and care and support. It impresses on the person the fact that he is not joined merely to a nameless, faceless universal church, but to a concrete company of persons whose names and faces one should know.

In my opinion, it would be going much too far to have the bishop snooping around asking the neighbors of the candidates for baptism (*competentes*) how they conduct themselves. Robert Grant told us that was the bishop's practice in fourth century Jerusalem after the candidates had turned in their names. On the First Sunday of Lent, apparently, his episcopal rounds were spiced with what seems to have been a considerable invasion of privacy.

As a former adult candidate for admission into communion with the Roman See, I cannot help thinking, however, that it would have been kind of nice to have had some slight indication, back in 1943, that the faith community I was joining was just a bit interested in me, even if it were manifest in prying. There was no prying, no snooping, and no apparent interest. Working with the warm bodies of one priest and one sponsor, I had to conjure up a church. Ralph Keifer's expression hit the nail on the head: "Yes, Virginia, there *is* a church."

In the new Roman *Rite of Christian Initiation of Adults*, this is one of the most obvious departures (and even repudiations) of our familiar patterns. Initiation comes through as a project of the concrete local church, a community process, in which the already initiated members of the church are as much involved as the candidates themselves.

A Church That Is Distinct and Different from the Culture

Just as significant for initiatory practice as our new attention to the local church, the concrete community of faith, is the painful shift back from a "Christendom" to a Christian mentality. Long after European and American cultures had liberated themselves from the domination of the ecclesiastical institutions, the mentality survived. It still survives in countless subtle ways.

It is, therefore, of critical importance that anyone concerned with Christian initiation should be absolutely clear that the church is distinct from any culture; that the church is neither identified nor identifiable with any culture; that the church is a sign community concerned with the transformation of the human person rather than with the conservation of the values of society.

This was one of the salient points of agreement in the initiation group at the Scottsdale meeting of liturgists in December of 1973. Fundamentally, it is merely another way of saying what Reginald Fuller said about Christian initiation in the New Testament.[4]

The identification of church and culture had become so complete in medieval Europe that Daniel Stevick correctly interpreted both Catholic and Reformed (and Anglican, as a combination of the two) ideas of confirmation, now separated from baptism, in the same way that one became a Christian by consenting to a pattern in his society, that in coming to terms ". . . with the values of society, he also came to terms with God and the Church."[5]

You can see what this does to the gospel notions of salt and light and leaven. It was hardly necessary to identify the believers any more. One just divided up the towns into parishes. Even when that situation ceased to exist in fact, it continued to reign in the habits of Christian thought, and worship, and life. Leonel Mitchell clearly demonstrated how all the churches of the Reformation period, with the possible exception of the Anabaptists, were pretty well caught in the same web.

The Second Vatican Council's break with that mindset was clear, although often stated gently. The introduction to the new Roman *Rite of Christian Initiation of Adults* quotes the council's *Decree on the Church's Missionary Activity:*

> . . . new converts set out on a spiritual journey. Already sharing through faith in the mystery of Christ's death and resurrection, they pass from the old man to the new one made perfect in Christ. This transition, which brings with it a progressive change of outlook and morals, should become evident together with its social consequences and should be gradually developed during the time of the catechumenate. Since the Lord in whom he believes is a sign of contradiction, the convert often experiences

human divisions and separations, but he also tastes the joy which God gives without measure.[6]

Ralph Keifer was not exaggerating when he described that initiatory rite as a "radical" reform, a reform which "on the one hand rejects the pastoral assumption that implicit faith is an acceptable standard for Christian life," and on the other hand demands a radical transformation of life and values.[7]

The point is not only that baptism, confirmation, and eucharist are again regarded as a continuum, belonging together, and celebrated normally at the Easter Vigil. The point is that these are the *sacraments* of initiation and that the *process* of initiation is far more extensive, including a precatechumenate or evangelization, a rite of becoming catechumens, an experiential catechumenate involving the whole local church, a rite of election of candidates for baptism, a Lenten period of purification and enlightenment in the midst of an assembly that is sharing prayer and faith and penance (the most intensive phase of catechesis), the celebration of the sacraments of initiation at Easter, and a period of postbaptismal catechesis until Pentecost.

This *process* is proposed again as normative, even though the *sacraments* of initiation continue to be celebrated for infants and children. This *norm* effectively shifts the focus of initiation from the individual to the community. What has been popularly regarded as a more or less private commerce between God and the human soul explodes into its full social dimensions. Grace and covenant come with incorporation into the community called church. Identification with the Lord is accomplished by the embrace of his band of disciples.

All this is necessary because the faith community is no pious facade for the world. It is not merely the world's "good" side, or the world's believing side. It is rather an agent of the kingdom, an agent of liberation and solidarity in God, a sign. It is salt and light and leaven again. It is not the picture of "Christendom" but a true gospel picture: a church that, while not alienated from the world, not withdrawn, not hostile, is quite distinct and different. Its members need the strength of joined hands and common faith to serve the human family as they must, in dialogue with the whole race and in a posture of critical covenant prophecy.

This is the way the church serves the world: not by confirming its ways and its values, but by challenging, and examining, and urging change in the light of the gospel. It is clear that this mission requires people who are converted, transformed, freed from the prisons of social status and role and custom.

A Church Whose Theology Follows From Its Life

Books outlast humans, and the written word is quite capable of exercising a tyrannical as well as a liberating influence. The written word is capable of holding in its sway generations to whose lives, conditions, desires, and needs it can no longer speak. That risk is the price we pay for inheriting the wisdom of the ancients and the Spirit's work in them.

But the Spirit is always present, always now, and tradition is a living reality which we are constantly creating as well as receiving. So books and formulas and texts must be modestly kept at the service of the living community of faith, responsive to its current situation and its real questions. It is one of the perennial and most serious temptations of the church to reverse this right order and put the living church in bondage to historical formulations. To be as God, to contain the holy, to package the holy, to somehow get the holy under our control—the prospect fascinates and tempts us whenever we forget our mortal limits.

Robert Grant described how theology and understanding emerged from the corporate life of the second century church: that the starting point of theology was found within the life of the community.[8]

Only the Lord is our God, and God is neither history's creature nor history's captive. Just as the assembly of persons is the most important symbol in Christian liturgical celebration, so the consensus of the living and contemporary church is the most trustworthy interpreter of the word of God. It is in life together that we gain understanding.

If that were not true, for example, the church today would still be baptizing only adults. It was out of our common life that we came to see the appropriateness of celebrating the *sacraments* of initiation with infants and children, even though the initiation *process* is essentially an adult experience. Unfortunately, the process got lost in the transition, partly because of the identification of church and culture discussed above. We must now recover it for the sake of the local church's character and identity.

Recovering the initiation process for adults, however, does not necessarily mean the repudiation of infant baptism-confirmation-eucharist. The Scottsdale liturgists' conference initiation group agreed that, while infant baptism derives from the adult form, it has a rationale: it places specific responsibilities upon the adult community, and when parents and congregation accept those responsibilities the celebration of infant baptism proclaims the initiative of God's love.

The resolutions of the same group suggested that "for children of responsible Christian parents" two different patterns of initiation might well coexist: the celebration of the sacraments of initiation (baptism, confirmation, eucharist) in infancy or childhood, to be followed by catechesis appropriate to succeeding stages of development; or the enrollment of the infant as a catechumen, with the sacraments of initiation to be celebrated at a later age, after catechesis.

Historical efforts to return to the practice of adult baptism only have not been terribly successful, both because such efforts fail to "interpret and support the place of the child in the church" and because "there is something normative about a child in the life of the kingdom."[9]

Like all sacraments, the sacraments of initiation are community celebrations and involve the whole assembly at Easter (and whenever else they are celebrated). Therefore the use of Lent as an annual period of intensive catechesis experience for the whole local church makes eminently good sense. Then the Easter Vigil can become what it is supposed to be: a real celebration of conversion, initiation, and commitment for everyone.

A Church That Is a Community of Lived Faith

A church conceived either as a place, sacred building, or as a hierarchy of clerical dispensers of grace for individuals is a church that has no need of initiation. Isn't that what has happened to us? We have seen what ensues when either of those notions become popularly accepted and even dominant. Scripture, creeds, and dogma to the contrary, if we listen carefully we will note that the word "church" is still used quite commonly in those dreadful ways.

It will take some doing and some years before "church" again means only people—and not just people or individuals with faith, but a common life in common faith. That is, people who share prayer, who share the problems of life, who share the exploration of Jesus' death-resurrection gospel, who share discipline, who share celebration, who share mission, and who therefore present a corporate and consensus moral and sign posture to the world.

But we cannot really expect "church" to mean these things until they become apprehendable and experiential realities in the life of most local churches. And they will become so only when at least a core group in each local church is enabled to feel the need for decision and commitment.

Ralph Keifer spoke of the present inability of the church to say "No" to anyone who presents himself for membership.[10] That inability is why we so desperately need an experiential catechesis or initiation process: to find out *in practice* whether people can learn to pray together, whether they can share problems and questions and insights, whether they can undertake the discipline of a common church life, etc. Then we will not have to ask questions. The answers will become clear in experience.

Then, too, we will be in a position at least to grapple with the other problem Keifer raised, namely, the impossibility of educating people to the values of a community unaware of itself as community.[11]

Eventually, a church that does something about a regular initiation catechesis experience for its members every Lent and Easter will find that it does have means to be a "reflective body with regard to issues of import outside the church door." It will no longer be in the position of merely exhorting its individual members to take private positions on political, economic, and other social questions. Its common prayer will bring it together and its common faith will lead it to preach the good news to the poor, to proclaim liberty to captives and new sight to the blind. It will speak to social questions as a community, respecting the limits of its competence, but with the boldness of faith and the Spirit.

A Church in Which People Are the "Primordial Sacramental Signs"

Ralph Keifer has stated that the new Roman *Rite of Christian Initiation of Adults* "represents a radical change of sacramental symbols and priorities . . . and a breathtaking departure from the recent past."[12] Just as it is a departure from the recent past, it is also a recovery of an earlier practice of catechesis and initiation in which persons were clearly the "primordial sacramental signs." The same shift in symbolism we see in the history of initiation practice (or lack of it) has been observed by students of the history of church architecture. Frédéric Debuyst comments on it in his *Modern Architecture and Christian Celebration.*[13] In the basilican period as well as in the earlier house-church period, the architecture of the place of ecclesial-liturgical assembly revealed, in Debuyst's opinion, that the person was the symbol par excellence. In succeeding ages, he notes a gradual shift from that personal symbolism to the more "objective" and material symbolism of the altar, other objects, and finally the church building itself. In contemporary times, the architecture of the place of assembly is again beginning to take cognizance of the symbolic primacy of the persons of the assembly.

Some Pastoral Inferences

The annual conferences sponsored by Notre Dame's Murphy Center have consistently dealt with key liturgical problems and have done so with careful scholarship, living faith, and pastoral sensitivity. It seems to me, however, that no theme of past years can match the potential of Christian initiation for a basic and practical impact on the life of the local church. Among the churches in communion with Rome, for example, this contribution, or its facsimile, is absolutely essential for a genuine pastoral implementation of the new *Rite of Christian Initiation of Adults* (as well as the 1969 rite for baptizing infants).

The papers presented at this conference represent a remarkable consensus on a number of important pastoral and practical problems. The writers of the papers drew some but not all of the conclusions or inferences which follow, so I do not ask them to assume the burden of my judgments. Readers can estimate the weight of the evidence for themselves.

The Unity of the Sacraments of Initiation

At least some of us in the initiation group at the Scottsdale conference in 1973 did not expect to have so much documentation for our first resolution provided so soon. The first resolution of the group stated that:

> The rite of Christian initiation should normally consist of a unified sacramental event in which the three now-separated moments (baptism, confirmation, eucharist) are integrated. The full rite should be used at any age when a person is initiated (i.e., infancy, childhood, or adulthood) . . . properly celebrated in the midst of the congregation.[14]

The rest of those resolutions are likewise substantiated by these proceedings. With regard to the unity of the rite, Nathan Mitchell spoke of the problem of "accumulated symbolism," pointing out how, when this becomes unlimited and undisciplined, the "basic architecture" of any rite "will begin to fracture."[15] His equally illuminating remarks about *anamnesis* and *epiclesis* as memory and invocation, about their dislocation, and about their replacement by terms of imitation and obedience, led him to conclude that this dislocation and replacement resulted in a view of initiation itself as imitative, and of the act of baptism as needing completion, or perfection, by a separate ritual act of confirmation.[16]

Daniel Stevick concluded his paper on initiatory practice after the Reformation just as emphatically:

> In sum, we have built questionable dynamics and motivations into our initiatory rites, and we have used bad arguments to show that it all made sense. It seems clear to me that theologically the sacramental parts of Christian initiation do not make sense except as elements in an intelligible unity standing for the indivisible whole of the redemptive mystery. Psychologically, it is selfdefeating to try to associate one part of this initiatory unity with one stage of life and other parts with other stages when no such staged-out meanings belong inherently to the rites themselves.[17]

Pastorally, the restoration of the integrity of the sacraments of initiation would mean that bishop or priest would baptize, confirm, and eucharistize candidates (whatever their ages) in one ritual action. It would emphasize again the ecclesial, corporate, congregational character of the rite and would help to reveal the nature of the church. It would require pastoral attention to the needs for conversion, death-resurrection, catechesis experiences at every stage of one's Christian life. It would solve the problem of a separate "confirmation" that seems to mean less as it is explained more. It would make more clear parental, family, and congregational responsibility for the nurture of Christian life. It would end the incongruous practice of baptizing someone and then immediately excommunicating him. It would offer the possibility of a clear and unambiguous reinitiation experience for the whole faith community each time these sacraments were celebrated (particularly at the Easter Vigil). It would provide the kind of sacramental framework or context in which an authentic adult catechumenate could have a chance of achieving the effects intended.

The Question of Episcopal Presidency

It is obvious that restoring the integrity of the rite means authorizing priests and deacons generally to confirm and to administer the eucharist when they baptize. Nathan Mitchell summarized the difference between East and West by stating that the East elected to maintain the unity of the initiation rite at the expense of episcopal presidency but the West chose to maintain episcopal presidency at the expense of ritual integrity.[18] This is why, with sufficient bishops around to preside, the sacraments of initiation remained integral and unified in the city of Rome until the twelfth century, long after they had disintegrated in most of the other sees of the West.

However, if priests generally are not to confirm, in order to make good ecclesial and pastoral sense, episcopal presidency in the sacraments of initiation should be reserved to *the* bishop of a diocese and should not be performed by anyone who happens to be in episcopal orders. Pastorally, too, it is terribly important that rites of initiation be celebrated in the concrete local church discussed above, in the assembly of those persons who constitute the church for the particular candidate.

I would not want to weaken in any way the tenuous hold which the episcopal office (in dioceses that are generally much too large) has on its pastoral and liturgical character. The church needs a much stronger sense of that character than it has possessed either with the administrator-bishop of the present or the prince-bishop of the past. Visiting parishes for a separated and disintegrated sacrament of "confirmation" has not been proven effective in promoting a healthier view of the episcopate. We do need, however, other ways to promote such a view and other means by which the bishop can become experientially present to the local church as pastor and liturgist, as agent of reconciliation and communion. But this is another subject, and one deserving lengthy treatment.

Pastorally, I think we can say that the restoration of the sacraments of initiation in their wholeness, with the presidency of either bishop or priest, does not deprive the episcopal office of any strong affirmation while it *does* make infinitely more sense out of the entire initiation process.

The Sacraments of Initiation as Community Event

Believing people identify themselves as church far more effectively through their experience than through textbooks, discussion groups, or reasoned argument. Pastorally, it seems to me, the celebration of baptism-confirmation-eucharist as a unified rite would facilitate this kind of ecclesial experience. Together, those sacraments speak of a God who does not dole out his mercy and loving kindness in a piecemeal and tantalizing fashion, but who freely makes us new and whole and complete at the very moment our lives are inserted into the paschal community and the paschal mystery.

If we are concerned about regaining a strong sense of the dignity of baptism and election, a strong sense of the priestly character of the people of God, and a consequent perspective and proportion with regard to particular offices and functions within the community of faith, then the restoration of the sacraments of initiation as community event and Easter celebration would seem to me to be a key prerequisite.

The Rediscovery of Lent and Easter

As long as confirmation is separated from baptism, it tends to offer the chimera of a magically sudden Christian maturity. With the restoration of a unified rite for the sacraments of initiation, we can hope that what the *Rite of Christian Initiation of Adults* presupposes will have a chance of pastoral implementation and realization: Lent as the climactic season of the catechumenate, when the whole community of faith enters into an intensive period of shared prayer, faith, discipline, rite, and mission; Easter as *the* celebration of the sacraments of initiation.

Whether the sacraments of initiation are celebrated with infants, or with children, or with adolescents, or with adults—and whether or not there are adult catechumens in any given Christian community—the community needs this annual experience of conversion, and commitment, and initiation. Lent is there waiting to be used. The Easter Vigil is there waiting still to be discovered as *the* Easter service, not some sort of prelude to the "masses of Easter Sunday."

Options for Christian Parents and Congregations

Under the heading "A Church Whose Theology Follows from Its Life," I mentioned these options: the celebration of baptism-confirmation-eucharist in infancy or childhood; or the enrollment of the infant or child as a catechumen, with the sacraments of initiation to be celebrated at a later age. The catechumen, as Aidan Kavanagh has stated forcefully, "is a Christian *in fieri* and a member of the church." Enrollment as a catechumen is already a real relation to Jesus Christ.

Perhaps a good deal of experimenting with these options is in order, despite what has been said above in defense of infant baptism. At the very least, recognition of these options as viable and acceptable in the parish can liberate us from the habit of rushing the infant from the hospital to the font as if God were counting the minutes. Aidan Kavanagh clarifies the meaning of "norm" in this connection:

> The Second Vatican Council set, in general, what the norms of the two premier events of the sacramental economy were to be. The *Constitution on the Sacred Liturgy* (41,42) states the *norm of the eucharist* to be a celebration presided over by the bishop surrounded by his people, presbyters, and other clergy. Even when circumstances require the bishop's physical absence such a celebration, being an act of the whole church, remains the norm. Underlying this norm is a theology that regards faith as a communal way of life knit together by events that are sacramental in nature and ecclesial in scope. Into such a faith lived communally baptism initiates one. The Council's stated *norm of baptism* could not have been one that was less sacramental in nature and ecclesial in scope.
>
> Thus in the dogmatic constitution of the church, *Lumen Gentium* (14), in the decree on the missionary activity of the church, *Ad Gentes* (13,14), and in the *Constitution on the Sacred Liturgy* (64–68), the norm of baptism was stated to be that of solemn initiation done at the paschal vigil and preceded by a catechumenate of serious content and some duration. These requirements suggest that the subject of initiation be an adult: indeed the conciliar emphasis is on the adult nature of the norm of Christian initiation, deriving as it does from the New Testament teaching on conversion. Nowhere does the Council deny the licitness of infant baptism. Nor does it deny the permissibility of the private low mass. But neither practice is vigorously defended either: even less is it suggested that infant baptism for initiation, or private low mass for the eucharist, be regarded as the normative modes of expressing these sacraments' place and importance in either the sacramental economy or the life of the church.[19]

On this last point of options, it is clear that we have much praying and sharing and experimenting to do before either will emerge as preferable. Perhaps neither will ever emerge as clearly preferable. But it seems to me that we have sufficient agreement on the first four pastoral inferences or conclusions to supply an agenda for a good long time. I can think of no agenda more important for a church that is seeking to renew its life and service.

NOTES

1. Cf. above, p. 32.
2. Cf. above, p. 2.
3. Cf. above, p. 73.
4. Cf. above, pp. 7–31.
5. Cf. above, p. 104.
6. "Decree on the Missionary Activity of the Church," #13 in *The Documents of Vatican II*, ed. by Walter M. Abbot (New York: Corpus Books, 1966): 599–600.
7. Cf. above, p. 139.
8. Cf. above, pp. 32–49.
9. Cf. above, p. 106.
10. Cf. above, p. 147.
11. Cf. above, p. 142.
12. Cf. above, p. 139.
13. Frederic Debuyst, *Modern Architecture and Christian Celebration*, eds. John G. Davies and George A. Raymond (Richmond, Va.: John Knox Press, 1968).
14. *Living Worship*, January 1974, The Liturgical Conference, Washington, D.C.
15. Cf. above, pp. 70–72.
16. Cf. above, pp. 73–75.
17. Cf. above, p. 116.
18. Cf. above, p. 52.
19. A. Kavanagh, "The New Roman Rite of Adult Initiation," *Studia Liturgica* 10 (1974): 35–47, esp. 36.

Bibliography

The following bibliography is neither extensive, nor does it contain all the works cited in the footnotes of this volume. It comprises primarily recent works in English, as well as a few of the standard classics, and is included here more for the guidance of those engaged in the practical field than for the research scholar. A fairly comprehensive bibliography of over 2,000 entries in all languages and covering all levels is available from the Murphy Center for Liturgical Research, University of Notre Dame.

Akeley, T. C. *Christian Initiation in Spain, C. 300–1100.* London: Darton, Longman and Todd, 1967.

Aland, Kurt. *Did the Early Church Baptize Infants?* Trans. by G. R. Beasley-Murray. Philadelphia: Westminster Press, 1963.

Araujo, Epaminondas. "Catecumenato Hoje." *Revista Eclesiastica Brasileira* 32 (1972): 582–589.

Armour, Rollin Stely. *Anabaptist Baptism.* Scottdale, Pennsylvania: Herald Press, 1966.

Arndt, Elmer J. F. *The Font and the Table.* Richmond, Virginia: John Knox Press, 1967.

Austin, Gerald. "The Essential Rite of Confirmation and Liturgical Tradition." *Ephemerides Liturgicae,* 86 (1972): 214–224.

Baillie, J. *Baptism and Conversion.* London: Oxford University Press, 1964.

Bailey, Derrick Sherwin. *Sponsors at Baptism and Confirmation.* London: SPCK, 1952.

Banting, H. M. S. "Imposition of Hands in Confirmation. A Medieval Problem." *Journal of Ecclesiastical History,* 7 (1956): 147–159.

Barth, Karl. *The Teaching of the Church Regarding Baptism.* Trans. by E. Payne. London: SCM Press, 1948.

Bartz, Wilhelm. *Orientierung über die Gültigkeit der Freikirchen und christlichen Sondergemeinschaften gespendeten Taufe.* Trier: Paulinus-Druckerei, 1971.

Baumgartner, Jakob. "Nach 1400 Jahren. Wiederbelerung des Katechumenats.

Zum neuen Ritus der christlichen Initiation Erwachsener." *Schweizerische Kirchenzeitung*, 140 (1972): 305–308, 323–326.

Beasley-Murray, G. R. *Baptism in the New Testament*. London: Macmillan & Company, Ltd., 1962.

———. *Baptism Today and Tomorrow*. London: Macmillan, 1966.

Bedard, Walter Maurice. *The Symbolism of the Baptismal Font in Early Christian Thought*. Studies in Sacred Theology, 2nd Series, Vol. 45. Washington: Catholic University of American Press, 1951.

Belcastro, Joseph. *The Relationship of Baptism to Church Membership*. St. Louis: Bethany Press, 1963.

Benning, Alfons. *Gabe des Geistes. Zur Theologie und Katechese des Firmasakramentes*. Kevelaer: Butzon en Bercker, 1972.

Beraudy, R. "Le Nouveau Rituel de l'Initiation Chrétienne." *Notes de Pastorale Liturgique* 100 (1972): 46–48.

Beraudy, Roger. "Recherches Theologiques autour du Rituel Baptismal des Adultes." *Maison-Dieu* 110 (1972): 25–50.

Biemer, G. *Die Firmung als Sakrament der Eingliederung in die Kirche. Theologische Grundliegung und pastorale Praxis*. Würzburg: Echter, 1973.

Biffi, Inos. 'Riflessioni Teologiche sul Nuovo 'Ordo Confirmationis'." *Rivista Liturgica* (Turin) 59 (1972): 313–323.

———. "Il Nuovo Rituale del Battesimo dei Bambini. Teologia e Riti." *Rivista del Clero Italiano* 51 (1970): 134–143.

Bleeker, C. J. *Initiation. Contributions to the Theme of the Study Conference of the International Association for History of Religions*. Strassbourg, 1964. Leiden: Brill, 1965.

Bleicher, Josef. "Bericht über ein Firmmodel." *Theologische Quartalschrift* 154 (1974): 77–80.

Blomfield, H. G. "Baptism and the Catechumenate." *Theology* 50 (1947): 129–131.

Borello, L. et al. *Educazione alla Fede e Iniziazione Cristiana. Atti del XV Convegno Liturgico-Pastorale*. Milano: Edizioni della Opera Regalità, 1973.

Botte, Bernard. "Problèmes de la Confirmation." *Questions Liturgiques et Paroissiales* 53 (1972): 3–10.

———. *Postbaptismal Anointings in the Ancient Patriarchate of Antioch*. The Syrian Churches Series 6. Ed. by Jacob Vellian. Kottayam: CMS Press, 1973: 63–71.

Bouyer, Louis. *Christian Initiation*. Trans. by J. R. Foster. New York: Macmillan, 1960.

Braganca, Joaquim O. "Le Symbolisme des Rites Baptismaux au Moyen Age." *Didaskalia* 3 (1973): 37–56.

Braniste, E. "L'Explication du Baptême dans les Catécheses de Saint Jean Chrysostome." *Studii Teologice* 22 (1970): 509–527.

Brock, Sebastian. *Consignation in the West Syrian Baptismal Rite*. The Syrian Churches Series 6. Ed. by Jacob Vellian. Kottayam: CMS Press, 1973: 100–110.

Brockett, Lorna. *The Theology of Baptism*. Theology Today Series, No. 25. Notre Dame, Indiana: Fides Publishers, 1971.

Brown, H. E. *Baptism through the Centuries*. Mountainview, California: Pacific Press Publications, 1965.

Bryce, Mary Charles. "The Catechumenate. Past, Present and Future." *American Ecclesiastical Review* 160 (1969): 262–273.

Burchill, G. S. "Some Questions on Confirmation." *Studia Liturgica* 4 (1965): 56–58.

Buswell, Charles A. "Pastoral Suggestions for the Celebration of Confirmation." *Worship* 46 (1972): 30–34.

Capelle, Bernard. "L'Introduction du Catéchumenat à Rome." *Revue de Theologie Ancienne et Medievale* 5 (1933): 129–154.

Caprile, G. "Il Nuovo Rito della Confirmazione." *Civiltà Cattolica* 122 (1971): 167–170.

Cattaneo, Enrico. "Il Nuovo Rito della Cresima. Una Svolta o un Ritorno?" *Rivista del Clero Italiano* 53 (1972): 398–405.

Cellier, Jacques. "Le Nouveau Rite de l'Initiation Chrétienne des Adultes." *Documentation Catholique* 54 (1972): 217–221.

——. "Le Baptême des Petits Enfants. Perspectives Actuelles de la Pastorale." *Notes de Pastorale Liturgique* 96 (1972): 4–8.

——. "Declaration des Évêques de France sur le Baptême des Petits Enfants." *Notes de Pastorale Liturgique* 96 (1972): 2–3.

Chavasse, A. "Histoire de l'Initiation Chrétienne des Enfants, de l'Antiquité à Nos Jours." *Maison-Dieu* 28 (1951): 26–44.

——. "Le Carême Romain et les Scrutins Prébaptismaux avant le IXe Siècle." *Recherches des Sciences Religieuses* 35 (1948): 325–381.

——. "La Discipline Romaine des Septs Scrutins Prébaptismaux. Sa Première Forme." *Recherches des Sciences Religieuses* 48 (1960): 227–240.

Christiaens, J. "L'Organisation d'un Catéchumenat au 16e Siècle." *Maison-Dieu* 58 (1959): 71–82.

Clark, Neville. "Christian Initiation. A Baptist Point of View." *Studia Liturgica* 4 (1965): 156–165.

Clercq, Paul de. "Réflexions Theologique sur la Confirmation." *Paroisse et Liturgie* 54 (1972): 294–301.

Connolly, R. H. "The Theology of Confirmation in Relation to Baptism." *Clergy Review* 27 (1947): 282–284.

Corvez, M. "Le Baptême des Enfants." *Nova et Vetera* 47 (1972): 138–140.

Coudreau, F. "The Catechumenate in France." *Worship* 42 (1968): 223–241.

Couratin, A. H. "Baptism. The Liturgical Pattern." *Church Quarterly Review* 157 (1956): 393–401.

Coventry, F. "Initiation Non Disintegrated." *Theology* 51 (1948): 68–69.

Crehan, J. *Early Christian Baptism and the Creed. A Study in Ante-Nicene Theology*. Bellarmin Series, Vol. 13. London: Burns Oates & Washbourne, 1950.

Crichton, J. D. "The New Confirmation Rite." *Life and Worship* 41 (1972): 14–16.

_____. "The Christian Initiation of Adults. A Pastoral Opportunity." *Life and Worship* 41 (1972): 8–12.

Cryer, Neville. *By What Rite?* London: A. R. Mowbray & Co. Ltd., 1969.

Cullman, Oscar. *Baptism in the New Testament.* Trans. by J. K. S. Reid. Studies in Biblical Theology, Vol. 1. London: SCM Press, 1950.

Cully, Kendig Brubaker (ed.). *Confirmation. History, Doctrine and Practice.* Greenwich, Connecticut: Seabury Press, 1962.

Davies, John Gordon. "The Disintegration of the Christian Initiation Rites." *Theology* 50 (1947): 407–412.

_____. *The Architectural Setting of Baptism.* London: Barrie and Rockliff, 1962.

Davis, Charles. *Sacraments of Initiation. Baptism and Confirmation.* New York: Sheed and Ward, 1964.

Degenhardt, J. J. (ed.). *Taufpastoral. Handreichung zur Vorbereitung und Spendung der Taufe.* Paderborn: Bonifacius, 1972.

Della Torre, Luigi. "Le Comunità Catecumenali." *Rivista di Pastorale Liturgica* 9 (1971): 512–515.

Dell'Oro, Ferdinando. *L' "Ordo Confirmationis" Romano-Franco-Germanico. Un Contributo alla Storia del Rito dal Secolo IX al Secolo XIII.* Aosta: Tipo-Offset Musumeci, 1972–1973.

Delorme, J. *Baptism in the New Testament.* Trans. by David Askew. London: Geoffrey Chapman, 1966.

Denyer, A. S. "Christian Initiation. A Methodist Note." *Studia Liturgica* 1 (1962): 191–193.

Dienst, Karl. *Moderne Formen des Konfirmandenunterrichts.* Gütersloh: Gerd Mohn, 1973.

Dix, Gregory. "The 'Seal' in the Second Century." *Theology* 51 (1948): 7–12.

_____. *The Theology of Confirmation in Relation to Baptism.* London: Dacre Press, 1946.

Dölger, Franz Josef. *Der Exorzismus im altchristlichen Taufritual. Eine religiongeschichtlichen Studie.* Studien zur Geschichte und Kultur des Altertums, Band 5, Heft 1–4. Paderborn: Schoeningh, 1909, reprint Johnson, 1967.

_____. *Sphragis. Eine altchristliche Taufbezeichnung in ihren Beziehungen zur profanen und religiösen Kultur des Altertums.* Studien zur Geschichte und Kultur des Altertums, Band 5. Paderborn, Schoeningh, 1911.

_____. *Das Sakrament der Firmung. Historisch-dogmatisch Dargestellt.* Theologische Studien der Österreichischen Leo-Gesellschaft. Vienna: 1906, reprint, Hildesheim: Gerstenberg, 1971.

Downing, J. "Reflexions on Christian Initiation." *Studia Liturgica* 1 (1962): 254–262.

Duchatelez, K. "L'Economie Baptismal dans l'Eglise Orthodoxe." *Istina* (Paris) 16 (1971): 13–36.

Dunn, J. D. G. *Baptism in the Holy Spirit. A Re-Examination of the New Testament Teaching on the Gift of the Holy Spirit in Relation to Pente-*

costalism Today. Studies in Biblical Theology, Series 2, Vol. 15. London: SCM Press, 1970, and Naperville, Illinois: Allenson, 1970.

Durand, Guy. "Quand Faut-Il Baptiser les Enfants?" *Liturgie et Vie Chrétienne* 71 (1970): 83–88.

Duval, Andre. "Le Concile de Trente et le Baptême des Enfants." *Maison-Dieu* 110 (1972): 16–24.

Edsman, C. M. "A Typology of Baptism in Hippolytus." *Studia Patristica* 2. Berlin: Akademie Verlag, (1957): 35–40. Texte und Untersuchungen, Vol. 64.

Edwards, O. C. "The Exegesis of Acts 8, 4–25 and Its Implications for Confirmation and Glossalalia. A Review Article of Haenchen's Acts Commentary." *Anglican Theological Review,* Supplementary Series, 2 (1973): 100–112.

Eliade, Mircea. *Rites and Symbols of Initiation.* Trans. by Willard R. Trask. New York: Harper and Row, 1966.

Eller, V. *In Place of Sacraments. A Study of Baptism and the Lord's Supper.* Grand Rapids: Eerdmans, 1972.

Every, George. *The Baptismal Sacrifice.* Studies in Ministry and Worship, Vol. 14. London: SCM Press, 1959.

Farnes, Pedro. "El Nuevo Ritual de la Confirmación." *Phase* 12 (1972): 219–236.

Fiala, Virgil E. "Der neue Ritus der Kindertaufe." *Erbe und Auftrag, Benediktinische Monatschrift* 48 (1972): 199–208.

Finn, Thomas. "Baptismal Death and Resurrection. A Study in Fourth Century Eastern Baptismal Theology." *Worship* 43 (1969): 175–189.

_____. *The Liturgy of Baptism in the Baptismal Instructions of Saint John Chrysostom.* Studies in Christian Antiquity vol. 15. Washington: Catholic University of America Press, 1967.

Finnegan, Eugene M. *The Origins of Confirmation in the Western Church. A Liturgical-Dogmatic Study of the Development of the Separate Sacrament of Confirmation in the Western Church Prior to the Fourteenth Century.* Diss. Fakultät Theologische Trier, 1970.

_____. *The Theology of Confirmation at the Time of Charlemagne.* Diss. Fakultät theologische Trier, 1968.

Fischer, Balthasar. "Neuordnung der Kindertaufe. Eine Letzter Zwischenbericht." *Gottesdienst* 5 (1971): 52–53.

_____. "Baptismal Exorcism in the Catholic Baptismal Rites after Vatican II." *Studia Liturgica* 10 (1974): 48–55.

_____. "Die Intentionen bei der Reform des Erwachsenen-und Kindertaufritus." *Liturgisches Jahrbuch* 21 (1971): 65–75.

Fisher, John Douglas Close. *Christian Initiation. Baptism in the Medieval West. A Study in the Disintegration of the Primitive Rite of Initiation.* Alcuin Club, Vol. 47. London: SPCK, 1965.

_____. *Christian Initiation. The Reformation Period. Some Early Reformed Rites of Baptism and Confirmation and Other Contemporary Documents.* Alcuin Club, Vol. 51. London: SPCK, 1970.

Gennep, Arnold van. *The Rites of Passage.* Trans. by Monika B. Vizedom and Gabrielle L. Caffee. Phoenix Books. Chicago: The University of Chicago Press, 1960.

Gignac, André (ed.). "Recherches Pratiques sur la Confirmation." *Liturgie et Vie Chrétienne* 83 (1973): 3–105.

Gilbert, W. Kent (ed.). *Confirmation and Education.* Yearbooks in Christian Education, Vol. 1. Philadelphia: Fortress Press, 1969.

Gilmore, Alec (ed.). *Christian Baptism. A Fresh Attempt to Understand the Rite in Terms of Scripture, History and Theology.* London: Lutterworth Press, 1959.

Guerrette, R. H. "The New Rite of Infant Baptism." *Worship* 43 (1969): 224–230.

Hanson, A. T. "Was There a Complementary Initiation Rite in the First Two Centuries?" *Theology* 75 (1972): 190–196.

Hatchett, Marion J. 'The Rite of 'Confirmation' in the Book of Common Prayer and in Authorized Services 1973." *Anglican Theological Review* 56 (1974): 292–310.

Hinchliff, Peter. "Baptism. The Third Dimension." *Theology* 73 (1970): 483–487.

Hines, John M. *By Water and the Holy Spirit.* Crossroad Book. New York: Seabury Press, 1973.

Hoekema, Anthony. *Holy Spirit Baptism.* Grand Rapids: Eerdmans, 1972.

Höslinger, Norbert. "Zum neuen Taufritus und sum Taufgespräch." *Bibel und Liturgie* 45 (1972): 177–179.

Holy Baptism. Supplement to Prayer Book Studies 26. New York: Church Hymnal Corporation, 1973.

Hughes, Philip Edgecombe. *Confirmation in the Church Today.* Grand Rapids: Eerdmans, 1973.

Hudson, W. D. "Christian Initiation. A Baptist Comment." *Studia Liturgica* 1 (1962): 69–73.

Hum, Jean Marie. "Renouveau de la Confirmation." *Notes de Pastorale Liturgique* 96 (1972): 9–15.

Huxtable, J. "Christian Initiation in Congregational Churches." *Theology* 55 (1952): 166–170.

Jagger, P. "An Anglican Reflection on the New Rite of Confirmation." *Life and Worship* 42 (1973): 17–23.

_____. "Baptism. The Ecumenical Sacrament." *Life and Worship* 40 (1971): 1–12.

_____. *Christian Initiation 1552–1969. Rites of Baptism and Confirmation Since the Reformation Period.* Alcuin Club, Vol. 52. London: SPCK, 1970.

Jeremias, Joachim. *The Origins of Infant Baptism.* Trans. by Dorothea M. Barton. Studies in Historical Theology, Vol. 1. London: SCM Press, 1963.

_____. *Infant Baptism in the First Four Centuries.* Trans. by David Cairns. Philadelphia: Westminster Press, 1962.

Johanny, Raymond. "Du Baptême à l'Eucharistie selon Saint Ambroise de Milan." *Parole et Pain* 9 (1972): 325–337.

Kavanagh, Aidan. "Initiation. Baptism and Confirmation." *Worship* 46 (1972): 262–275.

———. "The New Roman Rite of Adult Initiation." *Studia Liturgica* 10 (1973): 35–47.

———. "The Norm of Baptism: The New Rite of Christian Initiation of Adults." *Worship* 48 (1974): 143–152.

Keeman. A. "Blijvend Onbehagen in de Vormselpraktijk?" *Tijdschrift voor Liturgie* 56 (1972): 161–171.

Keifer, Ralph A. "Confirmation and Christian Maturity. The Deeper Issue." *Worship* 46 (1972): 601–608.

Kiesling, C. "The New Rite of Baptism for Children." *Cross and Crown* 24 (1972): 262–279.

Kirby, J. C. *Ephesians. Baptism and Pentecost.* Montreal: McGill University Press, 1968.

Kline, Meredith G. *By Oath Consigned. A Reinterpretation of the Covenant Signs of Circumcision and Baptism.* Grand Rapids: Eerdmans, 1968.

Küng, Hans. "Die Firmung als Vollendung der Taufe." *Theologische Quartalschrift* 154 (1974): 26–47.

Lampe, George William Hugo. *The Seal of the Spirit. A Study in the Doctrine of Baptism and Confirmation in the New Testament and the Fathers.* (2nd ed.) London: SPCK, 1967.

Lecuyer, J. "Rapport entre Foi et Baptême dans la Liturgie." *Ephemerides Theologicae Lovanienses* 49 (1973): 87–99.

Lengeling, Emil Joseph. "Vom Sinn des praebaptismalen Salbung." *Mélanges Liturgiques Offerts au R. P. Dom Bernard Botte à l'Occasion du Cinquantième Anniversaire de son Ordination Sacerdotale* (4 Juin 1972). Louvain: Abbaye du Mont César (1972): 327–358.

Lewandowski, Bogumil. Adnotationes Quaedam in Novum Ordinem Confirmationis." *Ephemerides Liturgicae* 86 (1972): 110–127.

Lewandowski, Bogumil. *Evolutio Ritus Liturgiae Confirmationis in Ecclesiis Occidentalibus.* Diss. Pontificio Instituto Liturgico, Rome, 1970.

Ligier, Louis. "La Prière et l'Imposition des Mains. Autour du Nouveau Rituel Romain de la Confirmation." *Gregorianum* 53 (1972): 407–486.

———. "La Confirmation en Orient et en Occident. Autour du Nouveau Rituel Romain." *Gregorianum* 53 (1972): 237–321.

———. *La Confirmation.* Theologie Historique, No. 23. Paris: Editions Beauchesne, 1973.

Llopis, Joan. "La Edad Para la Confirmación. Estado Actual del Problema." *Phase* 12 (1972): 237–248.

Lockton, W. "The Age for Confirmation." *Church Quarterly Review* 100 (1925): 27–64.

Lodi, Enzo. "Aspetti Pastorali dell 'Ordo Confirmationis.' " *Rivista Liturgica* (Turin) 59 (1972): 379–390.

_____. "Esperienze di Catecumenato Prebattesimale." *Rivista di Pastorale Liturgica* 9 (1971): 24–40.

Lottman, Ignace. "Een Doopviering." *Rond de Tafel. Liturgisches Tijdschrift* 27 (1972): 49–53.

Lotz, Johannes. "Zur Frage der Kindertaufe. Eine anthropologische Überlegung." *Trierer Theologische Zeitschrift* 80 (1971): 110–121.

Marravee, W. "Confirmation. A Conflict between Theology and Practice." *Eglise et Theologie* (1972): 221–238.

Marsh, Thomas. "A Study of Confirmation." *Irish Theological Quarterly* 39 (1972): 149–163, 319–336.

_____. "A Study of Confirmation. III." *Irish Theological Quarterly* 40 (1973): 125–147.

Maur, Hansjoerg auf der (ed.). *Zeichen des Glaubens Studien zur Taufe und Firmung. Festschrift Balthasar Fischer.* Freiburg im Breisgau: Herder, 1972.

McCarthy, Joseph M. "The Pastoral Practice of the Sacraments of Cleansing in the Legislation of the Visigothic Church." *Classical Folia* 24 (1970): 177–186.

McManus, Frederick. "Ritual of Infant Baptism." *American Ecclesiastical Review* 160 (1969): 190–199.

McReavy, L. L. "Notes on Roman Documents. The Matter and Form of Confirmation." *Clergy Review* 57 (1972): 141.

Miller, Ronald H. *Enlightenment through the Bath of Rebirth. The Experience of Christian Initiation in Late Fourth Century Jerusalem.* Diss. Fordham University, 1972.

Milner, Austin P. *Theology of Confirmation.* Theology Today Series, No. 26. Notre Dame, Indiana: Fides Publishers, 1971.

Mitchell, Leonel Lake. *Baptismal Anointing.* Alcuin Club, Vol. 48. London: SPCK, 1966.

_____. *Four Fathers on Baptism. Saint John Chrysostom, Saint Ephraem, Theodore of Mopsuestia, Narsai.* The Syrian Churches Series 6. Ed. by Jacob Vellian. Kottayam: CMS Press, 1973: 37–56.

_____. "What is Confirmation?" *Anglican Theological Review* 55 (1973): 201–212.

_____. "The Shape of the Baptismal Liturgy." *Anglican Theological Review* 47 (1965): 410–418.

_____. "Revision of the Rites of Christian Initiation in the American Episcopal Church." *Studia Liturgica* 10 (1974): 25–34.

Molin, Jean Baptiste. "Il Nuovo Rituale della Iniziazione Cristiana degli Adulti." *Revista Liturgica* (Turin) 60 (1973): 447–457.

_____. "Rituale della Iniziazione Cristiana degli Adulti." *Rivista Liturgica* (Turin) 60 (1973): 458–511.

Moreton, Michael. "The Emergence and the Forms of a Rite of Initiation in the Church." *Theology* 75 (1972): 41–47.

Moss, Basil S. (ed.). *Crisis for Baptism*. Living Church Books. London: SCM Press, 1965.

Neunheuser, B. *Baptism and Confirmation*. Trans. by J. J. Hughes. New York: Herder and Herder, 1964.

Newns, Brian. "Liturgical Bulletin. The New Ordo Confirmationis." *Clergy Review* 57 (1972): 41–47.

———. "Liturgical Bulletin. The Ordo Baptismi Parvulorum." *Clergy Review* 54 (1969): 703–710.

———. "Liturgical Bulletin. The New Rite for Infant Baptism." *Clergy Review* 54 (1969): 54–59.

———. "The Ordo Initiationis Christianae Adultorum." *Clergy Review* 57 (1972): 938–948.

Nocent, Adrien. "Vicissitudes du Rituel de la Confirmation." *Nouvelle Revue Theologique* 94 (1972): 705–720.

Ollard, L. "Confirmation in the Anglican Communion." *Confirmation or the Laying on of Hands*, Vol. 1. New York: Macmillan, 1926, p. 62f.

O'Reilly, J. O. "The Age—or Stage—for Confirmation." *Clergy Review* 55 (1970): 229–233.

Oriol, Joan. "El Nuevo Ritual de la Confirmación." *Phase* 12 (1972): 169–178.

Pepperdene, Margaret. "Baptism in the Early British and Irish Churches." *Irish Theological Quarterly* 22 (1955): 110–123.

Perrey, David G. *Baptism at 21*. New York: Vantage Press, 1974.

Perry, Michael Charles. *Crisis for Confirmation*. London: SCM Press, 1967.

Pocknee, Cyril E. *Baptism and Confirmation Today*. St. Charles Booklet Library. Tracts for the Times, No. 2. London: League of Anglican Loyalist, 1969.

———. "The Archaeology of Baptism." *Theology* 74 (1971): 309–310.

———. *Water and the Spirit*. London: Darton, Longman and Todd, 1967.

Porter, H. Boone. "Baptism: Its Paschal and Ecumenical Setting." *Worship* 42 (1968): 205–214.

Pryke, J. "The Sacraments of Holy Baptism and Holy Communion in the Light of the Ritual Washings and Sacred Meals at Qumran." *Revue de Qumran* 5 (1965–66): 543–552.

Puttmann, E. "The Rite of Baptism. Pastoral Aspects." *Life and Worship* 39 (1970): 11–13.

Putz, J. "The New Rite of Confirmation." *Clergy Monthly* (1972): 106–113.

Quasten, Johannes. "The Garment of Immortality. A Study of the 'Accipe Vestem Candidam.'" *Miscellanea Liturgica in Onore di sua Eminenza il Cardinale Giacomo Lercaro* 1. Roma: Desclée et Cie, 1966: 391–401.

———. "Baptismal Creed and Baptismal Act in St. Ambrose's *De Mysteriis* and *De Sacramentis*." *Melanges Joseph de Ghellinck, S.J.*, (Museum Lessianum—Section Historique, No. 13) Gembloux: Editions J. Duculot, S.A., 1951: 223–234.

Reckinger, Franz. " 'Accipe Signaculum.' Die Firmung in neuer Gestalt."
Heliger Dienst 26 (1972): 164– 174, and 27 (1973): 13–23.

Redmond, Richard. "Infant Baptism. History and Pastoral Problems." *The-ological Studies* 30 (1969): 79–89.

Repp, Arthur Christian. *Confirmation in the Lutheran Church.* Saint Louis: Concordia Publishing House, 1964.

Riley, Hugh. *The Rite of Christian Initiation. A Comparative Study of Interpretation of the Baptismal Liturgy in the Mystagogical Writings of St. Cyril of Jerusalem, St. John Chrysostom, Theodore of Mopsuestia and Ambrose of Milan.* Diss. Fakultät Theologische Regensburg, 1971.

Rotelle, John. "The Commemoration of Baptism in the Life of a Christian." *Ephermerides Liturgicae* 86 (1972): 474–485.

Ryder, Andrew. "Parents' Faith and Infant Baptism." *Clergy Review* 58 (1973): 746–759.

Schnackenburg, Rudolf. *Baptism in the Thought of St. Paul. A Study in Pauline Theology.* Oxford: Basil Blackwell, 1964.

Senn, F. C. "Confirmation and First Communion. A Reappraisal." *Lutheran Quarterly* 23 (1971): 178–191.

Shepherd, Massey H. "Confirmation. The Early Church." *Worship* 46 (1972): 22–29.

Siefer, Gregor. "Initiation aus der Sicht des Soziologen." *Theologische Quar-talschrift* 154 (1974): 10–25.

Stevick, Daniel B. "Types of Baptismal Spirituality." *Worship* 47 (1973): 11–26.

Suttner, Ernst Christoph. "Taufe und Firmung." *Regensburger Ökumenisches Symposion,* Vol. 2. Regensburg: Pustet, 1971.

Talec, Pierre. "Le Baptême. Pour quel Homme?" *Parole et Pain* 9 (1972): 88–95.

Thornton, L. S. *Confirmation. Its Place in the Baptismal Mystery.* West-minster: Dacre Press, 1954.

Tugwell, Simon. "Reflections on the Pentecostal Doctrine of 'Baptism in the Holy Spirit.' " *Heythrop Journal* 13 (1972): 268–281.

Turck, A. "Aux Origines du Catéchumentat." *Revue des Sciences Philoso-phiques et Théologiques* 48 (1964): 20–31.

Veilleux, Gaston. "Histoire des Développements Récents de la Pastorale du Baptême des Enfants." *Liturgie et Vie Chrétienne* 80 (1972): 8–22.

Vernette, P. "Le Catéchumenat en France." *Documentation Catholique* 54 (1972): 222–223.

Violle, Bernard. "Problèmes Pastoraux de la Confirmation en France." *Maison-Dieu* 110 (1972): 72–87.

Wagner, G. *Pauline Baptism and the Pagan Mysteries.* Trans. by J. B. Smith. Edinburgh: Oliver & Boyd, 1967.

Wagner, Johannes (ed.). *Adult Baptism and the Catechumenate.* Concilium. Theology in the Age of Renewal 22, New York: Paulist Press, 1967.

Wainwright, Geoffrey. "The Baptismal Eucharist before Nicea. An Essay in Liturgical History." *Studia Liturgica* 4 (1965): 9–36.

———. "The Rites and Ceremonies of Christian Initiation." *Studia Liturgica* 10 (1974): 2–24.

———. *Christian Initiation.* Ecumenical Studies in Theology, Vol. 10. London: Lutterworth Press, 1969.

Whitaker, Edward Charles. *Documents of the Baptismal Liturgy* (2nd ed.) London: SPCK, 1970.

———. *The Baptismal Liturgy.* Studies in Christian Worship, Vol. 5. London: The Faith Press. 1965.

———. "The History of the Baptismal Formula." *Journal of Ecclesiastical History* 16 (1965): 1–12.

Willoughby, Harold Rideout. *Pagan Regeneration. A Study of Mystery Initiations in the Graeco-Roman World.* Chicago: University of Chicago Press, 1960.

Wilson, W. G. "Christian Initiation." *Church Quarterly Review* 158 (1957): 21–38.

Yarnold, E. "Baptism and the Pagan Mysteries in the Fourth Century." *Heythrop Journal* 13 (1972): 247–267.

Yarnold, Edward. *The Awe-Inspiring Rites of Initiation. Baptismal Homilies of the Fourth Century.* London: St. Paul's Publications, 1971.

Young, Frank Wilbur. *Initiation Ceremonies. A Cross-Cultural Study of Status Dramatization.* Indianapolis: Bobbs-Merrill, 1965.

Ysebaert, Joseph. *Greek Baptismal Terminology. Its Origins and Early Development.* Graecitas Christianorum Primaeva, Vol. 1. Nijmegen: Dekker & Van de Vegt, 1962.

Index

179